The Widow Lessons

By Bridget Clawson

1

Dedication

Thank you to my family and friends for helping me write this book, as I learned how to live.

Family:

Ben, Kristen, Ewan Clawson; Andy, Sara, Julian, Bella and Theo Clawson; Caroline, Scott, Luke, Lily Darrow.

Friends:

Susan, my dearest friend, smart and strong.

Dani – World Champion with horses and me…and a lot of other things, too.

Guide:

Starla Bressler – my grief counselor, my guide.

The Widow Lessons

It was the afternoon of a day in February 2008 when I received a phone call at work from my husband, Ted. He was asking for a ride the next day so that he could go to the hospital and have a biopsy of an unusual something found near his liver and pancreas on an MRI he had taken to locate possible gall bladder stones. I will always look back on that day as a cruel and ordinary day when everything I loved was shattered irrevocably. A diagnosis of stage four pancreatic cancer followed soon after the biopsy. Ted was dead thirteen months later.

We married when I was nineteen and he was twenty-six. We literally had nothing except two dogs named Stubby and Milly and a 1957 Chevy pickup, the kind with the wrap around rear window. I became Mrs. Ted Clawson and we built our own little world over the course of thirty-four years, and it belonged to us alone. We were each other's exclusive be all everything….with three exceptions – our three children, all grown up and on their own by the time of Ted's diagnosis. The five of us Clawson's were enough for Ted and me. All there was or need be. Everything.

We fought Ted's cancer and we also fought to keep our equilibrium, our normal life. Fighting cancer has been described as a knife fight in the darkest alley. This awful and relentless fight changed how Ted and I lived, even as we continued and sometimes forced the daily rituals we had composed over a lifetime together.

Our fight against Ted's cancer ended in his death. Part of me knew that he was dying but part of me felt certain that I could save his life with a new procedure just on the market. Many times I was crouched in our bathroom while I covered my mouth with my cupped hand, secretly arranging treatments with various oncology centers. I know now that while I was skulking in the bathroom trying to save his life, Ted was talking privately in the living room with his Hospice nurse about how to die.

Ted and I shared everything with each other before cancer. Now, neither one of us was talking to the other about dying or not dying. I feel profound sadness about that. I guess you could say we each started lying to one another toward the end of Ted's life. I realize now that Ted knew he was dying and could only talk with his Hospice nurse about it, and not me. That's a hard thing to look at. To live with.

Regret is a key component in the deep pain of grief. For me, it visited early and it visited often. It felt unbearable at times, like being buried alive.

Today, I enjoy being alive most days, followed by the next day, and the next. And yet, in each day after day after day there is still a rambling, roaming search for the way forward alone in a world where some of the personal rhythms of my life before Ted's cancer and death simply don't work or fit.

I kept and still keep a journal. I hope other widows will, too. It helps. I look back every now and then, and I can see how I have learned, grown, tried and failed…and tried again.

This day – whichever day it happens to be in the unstoppable procession of days – I am learning how to be a widow.

Shock

Ted slid into a deep, drug-induced coma in the days before he took his last breath. He died at home in our bed. Whenever I think of that fact – that he died in our bed, in our home – I feel happy for him. He wanted to die at home and not have to go to a hospital. He got that wish, at least. What a strange consolation, I thought at the time. Later, I would have a new perspective.

I also recall that from the moment I realized that he had truly breathed his final breath, I felt very little inside other than a cavernous void. I felt like an empty, high-ceilinged warehouse.

His soul and spirit were no longer in his body. This I knew. I walked into our room over and over and gazed upon his dead body. I wandered around in what felt like a house of mirrors. I was everywhere and I was lost, both at the same time. It was harrowing, surreal, dull, numbing, hollow and disorienting. When I moved around, it felt like I was buried alive, lumbering around underground where everything seemed strangely familiar, only without adequate lighting.

When the funeral home came to transport Ted's body, I let it go with ease. Maybe I was even angry with his body, for letting such a thing happen to my friend. My love. I don't know. Would I ever learn to live with a spiritual presence that took no earthly form? Or – as I would discover later – perhaps there is a physical connection.

I was in shock. I now know first-hand that profound grief affects every sense, and can be disorienting. It's not a good idea to drive yourself, or chop wood, etc., since your right hand isn't speaking to your left hand at the moment. And no part of you is speaking with your rational mind. Staying pretty close to home base is a good idea. I was barely able to boil water without burning the house down. My short term memory was in a coma.

Wherever a new widow can find her bearings, find comfort, she should spend time there. It may be home. It may be a friend's house. It doesn't matter. She should try and spend as much time as possible in her personal, private comfort zone….even if it is deep inside her own heart.

I had to wander around the house a lot to find out that my only sanctuary was in quiet moments with myself, at home, on my couch near my dogs. There I sunk.

Shock does not last forever. But it did visit me intermittently, for a long time. I don't know when or if it will return.

Tasks

I was mechanically alive and in touch with some of the things I needed to do in order to process the implications of Ted's death, so to speak. We had three dogs who were grief stricken and confused. I had to care for them and try to explain what had happened, although they undoubtedly already knew. Maybe I was trying to get them to tell me what *they* knew.

We also had a cat that once belonged to our daughter, Caroline. He was acting even more smug than usual which caused me to like him both more and less. I recall feeling consciously responsible for the dogs and the cat, whereas before caring for them was more of an automatic part of my daily routine. Perhaps having them in my care was a mercy, as each task was a chance to think about something other than the pain and confusion I felt, my grief.

I hope that every widow finds this kind of outlet available. It really is a mercy to have little creatures, a house, or garden – something you can cling to and care for in your grief. It's like a salve for your deepest wounds.

There are frustrations in the outside world that you will undoubtedly encounter. You have to fill out form after form once you become a widow. For me, Bank of America was the worst. They lost death certificates and they took the wrong name off of documents, just to state a few of the multitude of errors. I learned that the bigger the organization, the more they do not talk to each other within that organization.

Everyone at every turn wanted an original death certificate – banks, lenders, governments. I advise every widow to order a dozen original death certificates. For years after Ted's death, I occasionally needed yet another one. Some get returned and some don't.

One of the worst parts of the early days as a widow is the new reality you and you alone are trapped in – how can all these other people be chatting and carrying on as if nothing has happened! Why can't anybody fix this? In my life, all these strangers I had to deal with were acting as if Ted's dying was normal and sad, but okay. No! I wanted to scream. It is not okay.

Among the many practical problems I faced, I had to figure out where to sleep while a new bed arrived and new carpet was installed in our bedroom. I had to get up in the mornings because of the dogs. I had paperwork chores at the bank, at Social Security and so forth. Every day I added something to my conveyor belt of things to focus on besides my bereavement.

For some widows, it may take a long time before tackling the tasks of daily life even seems possible. For me, staying busy was my way of enduring the horrible pain of grief.

I advise anyone experiencing grief to not "choose" how to be or feel based on perceived virtue. Be yourself. Do as you feel like doing. Do what you want to do. All of your energy is used in grieving, no matter your chosen way.

Spring was beginning and our home was on acres of woods, so I had raking and pruning and washing and burn piles to tend. Normally, I would have been excited about spring. Now, everything was a rote task.

Intermittently, a wave of grief would double me over and I wailed uncontrollably. When this happened, I had no choice but to just sit down and listen the way an abandoned house might listen to the sound of its own doorbell ringing. Grief was running the show.

Hospice grief counselors were busy with me. Some of the suggestions and concepts I learned from one particular grief counselor, Starla, saved me from madness I believe. I hung on her words, because I needed to be soothed and because much of what she was saying rang true for me. I see now how hard she and I were both working to teach me how to be in the new world that I now inhabited, against my will.

Taking advantage of Hospice grief counselors was the best step I ever could have taken. My grief counselor, Starla Bressler, was a god-send for me. She led me through the darkest moments of my loss and separation from Ted. For me, being a widow also meant utter separation from my familiar self, and I needed a guide.

Shame and Guilt

The memorial service for Ted was held at the roll call trailer for the road maintenance workers of Snohomish County in Arlington, Washington. This is where Ted had worked for many years. Ted had asked our son, Andy, to take charge of a memorial. Brother, Ben and sister, Caroline helped Andy and the three of them did all the work and planning.

Ben is the eldest, tall and broad shouldered. He has a sharp and literal mind, a protector, a go-to guy, a former marine (although once a marine, always a marine). If there is a proper way to do a thing, that will be Ben's way. Ben looks at home in the big chairs of his father.

Andy is the second. He's lanky with a sincere and clever ease. His is a versatile mind – musician, actor, idealist, experimenter, and teacher. His life unfolds as a series of meaningful quests. He and his father listened to all kinds of music with a shared heart.

Caroline is third. She is a quick-minded perfectionist and introvert. She has her father's smile, his procrastination, and moments of his sharp tongue – although, like him, she reserves more than she gives. She wrangles with outrage against injustice while simultaneously not wanting to ruffle any feathers along the way.

All three are eager to show kindness to any stranger. They are strong and hard-working. Their collective belief during their father's illness was that nothing could ever take their father. He was as invincible as he was fun. I know now they love me, the organizer of the family. I didn't always know it.

To design the memorial, they raided my photo stash and found some emblematic images of their own childhood. Anyone who saw the photo collection could plainly see that Ted was at the center of their lives, and mine.

I didn't participate at all in the mechanics of the service. I attended in a black jacket and slacks with a blouse of lavender, Ted's favorite color. My body was still and my mind was ice and I didn't speak.

After watching the kids pull together a satisfying and heart-felt memorial for their dad, I recommend any widow to consider letting trusted others take charge of your loved one's funeral or memorial. The organizational skills required are all-consuming. It takes a team of loving family and/or friends who are up to the task. As a new widow, you probably aren't qualified. I know I wasn't.

I also discovered that mourning and grief are two different things. Mourning is about your outward expression of loss. Grief is about how you feel. I know now that choosing Ted's favorite color to wear had meaning as an expression of mourning. I now have a bracelet that I always wear. Some people chose to continue wearing their wedding band, as an expression of mourning. Queen Victoria mourned in many ways, including forever wearing black and setting the table for Albert at every meal.

I think back on that service and remember feeling proud and impressed by our kids. I remember hoping that everything went along in a way that would do Ted justice. I certainly wanted everyone to know what a cataclysmic loss our family had suffered. But, in truth, I still hadn't faced the finality of Ted's death. So, everything I remember about the memorial seems akin to a strange, dark play that the kids were all in.

I realize now that I wanted to think the audience looked upon me and my family with sympathy. To me at that time, it made sense that if I got sympathy, then the whole play would be complete and Ted and I could go home. In my imagination, we would have talked all the way home in the car about what great people our little babies had become.

I remember feeling physically stiff at Ted's memorial, like one of those cardboard cops designed to remind shoppers not to steal. I also recall slouching down in my metal, folding chair, with my arm wrapped around my daughter's arm. I tried to make myself small – something I unconsciously do when I am somewhere I don't want to be.

The memorial was well-attended and it was my first realization of how frightening it was to be around people without Ted with me. I felt transformed somehow by his death in a way that made me feel stripped bare. I didn't want anyone to see me this way.

At some point I realized it was humiliating at a deep, deep level that I had let Ted die. I wanted to be far away from the human race because I had failed.

Shame and guilt are close kin emotions that may intermittently appear as part of the torture of grief. They were my early, constant companions. If you are feeling this way, I want you to know that after a period of time has passed, these feelings will take on a deeper, more constructive meaning.

Dreams

While my bedroom got converted from a hospital room to a bedroom again, I slept in the spare room. I had dreams and nightmares mixed with tossing and turning. The night of the memorial service, I had a particularly revealing nightmare.

In this vivid dream, Ted and I were kidnapped in our driveway. The head kidnapper did all the talking. "If you do what we say, no one will be hurt." We stayed with our captors during cold days and hot days. In my dream, we had a swimming pool and we all swam together – Ted, me and the kidnappers. I could smell the chlorine and I wondered to myself as I swam if I would be asked to maintain the pool, or if the kidnappers were going to do that forever. Everything was going pretty smoothly – one man helped me in the garden by picking string beans and killing slugs. The lead man played cribbage with Ted and made Ted laugh a lot the way he does when he's drinking beer. Then, one of our captors murdered Ted in a slow and painful, strangely silent and bloodless way, in our bed. "You can go now," the lead kidnapper said to me in a cheery tone. "Have a nice life." I never got a look at his face.

After that dream, I started keeping a note card and a pen by my bed. That particular dream made me realize how betrayed I felt. I was also looking for clues, for instructions – anything that would help me get Ted back, in whatever shape or form. I wrote down my dreams from that point forward.

This helped me look at things deeply at the time, and much later, too.

I think it's important to look for answers. At first, it's probably going to be about making time reverse itself. Or correcting this impossible thing that has happened. But looking for answers is an important part of healing your body, mind and spirit, and learning to live again.

Dreams and nightmares can be roadmaps inside your heart as well as your head. Use them for understanding. That understanding will probably, in time, provide some measure of peace.

Finding Comfort

The generous people attending Ted's memorial brought loads upon loads of beautiful food. The kids were hosting a wake in Seattle with their own friends later that night, and so they put the leftover memorial food into the back of my Outback in order to transport it to my house. The plan was for Andy to move all the food from my car to various other people's cars and head south to Seattle around 6 that evening.

My children's pain and grief was very different from my own. They needed their own comfort and rituals. I realized this much later as I was a witness to some of what each was going through. There was no shortage of suffering, confusion and deep sadness. I don't think anyone can ever completely know the depths of sorrow someone else is experiencing.

Someone at the memorial service had put a crumpled beer can in with the food, either as an homage to Ted -- who was a well-known beer drinker-- or perhaps as a strange statement of derision about the entire situation. Maybe it was an enemy who resented all the attention and love pouring out for Ted. I'll never know.

What I do know is that when I reached inside to pick the can up and toss it into the garbage, I cut the middle finger of my right hand on the lip of the can, and blood began to bead up at the fingertip. I hungrily sucked on it all the way home. I felt strangely nourished by this primal action, the way a child sucks her thumb when she is terrified.

This sucking of my finger, of my blood, seems strange to me now. On the other hand, it's a good representation of what was going on with me. Everything about grief is primal. And who else did I have now, except for myself? Was I still real?

Some cultures incorporate self-mutilation into grieving rituals. This includes suicide, amputations, head-bashing and starvation, just to name a few. I wasn't self-mutilating, but I can now understand the metaphor. I also know that profound grief and the strong reactions to it know no geographical or cultural bounds.

The best advice I have for the bereaved is to take care of yourself, however and whatever that may mean, moment-to-moment. Accept all of your reactions as your mind, body and spirit are trying to right themselves, and find balance and comfort.

Finding a Letter

Early days after Ted's death were terrible times of being and not being. Death had taken the one I love away from me by means of an amputation of sorts. I mentally and emotionally limped around my house. Shock was wearing off.

The next set of emotions I can only describe as a kind of cleaning up, tidying things urge. I saw many belongings of Ted's that I wanted to let go of – as in burn, throw away, give away or donate.

For example, Ted had approximately two hundred cribbage boards that I would need to sort out. If you are familiar with cribbage, there are some famous makers, such as Cooks and an infinite variety of types, materials and styles. Cribbage is played all over the world.

Ben was the first of the kids to comb through the board collection. He took the Cooks boards, and the one designed to travel on a ship. Later, Andy and Caroline would want some too. I kept the ones Ted loved the most for myself. These included a scrimshaw, a walrus jawbone and some quirky, homemade boards.

"You liked the simplicity of cribbage I think, and you liked that it stood the test of time," I said aloud to Ted as I gathered all the remaining boards into one place a few days after the memorial.

To widows, my advice about possessions is for you to keep everything you want for yourself, with the exception of wishes expressed in the last will. Talk with your kids about your own wishes about things, stuff, possessions, etc.

In my case, I let the kids know that I would gradually be putting everything I didn't want to keep in an outbuilding. During visits they could go there and take whatever they like.

I asked for no squabbling. Either they have obeyed my wishes, or argued but spared me the details. At any rate, I asked and I received. So, my advice is to ask.

Ted had stored many of the more common cribbage boards under our bed. One day, I was on my hands and knees, windshield wiping everything out from under there with the handle of an old broom. Tangled up in the dog hair and dust bunnies that I had swiped out from under the bed, I found a list Ted wrote and gave to me once.

We used to deal with things through writing and exchanging lists and letters. Therefore, I knew that while he was writing this note to me, I would have been writing one to him. But mine wasn't under the bed. Just his was. I was instantaneously euphoric to see his handwriting! It was almost like a Ted kiss on the Bridget cheek. He wrote on Xerox paper with blue ink. I copy it here, with all of its original punctuation and sentence structure problems:

1. When you are upset with someone or something else don't pick a fight with me so you will have a handy or manageable focus for your anger.

2. When you get a burst of "do it now" energy go on and do it now don't use the energy to delegate and manage tasks for others who must do it at your direction.
3. When you start to criticize and nitpick before you speak your mind run it through your mind and decide what your response would be if someone made a similar criticism of you, expect the same response from your target.
4. When you get an "ah ha" about something you wish to do about TV etc. just do it but don't expect everyone else to copy you.
5. While you are demanding to be accepted for yourself don't forget to accord other people the same respect.
6. When other people are having a discussion about you and not with you leave them alone unless they invite you into the conversation.
7. Practice using the pronouns we, us, and our instead of I, me and my whenever possible.
8. Whenever possible use plain English to say what you mean rather than jargon and buzz words that are of no use to people wrestling with real problems.
9. Learn patience. When you are ready someone else may not be and it is ok for them to not be ready!!!

Finding this lost letter was my first reminder that our marriage was not without conflict. It was actually a relief to remember that our marriage was lively, emotional and difficult at times. It was real.

I strongly believe now that the way you feel about your marriage has no bearing on grief. You can have a love/hate relationship with someone and that has no bearing on grief when that someone is taken from this world. Grief is about separation, love, and loss -- not the level of perfection in the relationship.

I rubbed the Ted letter with the palm of my hand, and said aloud, "That's the only time I think you ever used exclamation points. I wish you were writing me a to-do list today."

At that moment, I smiled…and I felt a feeling that can only be described as an internal certainty that Ted was smiling back at me. Maybe there is a physical connection, however elusive.

Slowly, after he died, I felt Ted's presence more and more in my life. I talked with him. I was beginning to feel his response. I felt connected. I have heard others say the same thing about their late husbands. I now understand that it is true.

Starla

Starla, the grief counselor from Hospice assigned to me, came to see me at 12:30 one day during the cribbage board roundup time. Starla is a nice lady, a bit younger than me, dark hair, on the quiet side and very smart. Hospice sent her to check on me.

I whisked her into the living room and closed the door behind us so the dogs wouldn't sniff her to death. She said she was a dog person. I knew it was probably lunch time in the outside world, but I didn't have any food in the house that wasn't half rotten, so I didn't offer her food.

I told Starla about the kidnap dream. We talked about how angry I felt that the kidnappers had gone back on their word. I felt like "having hope" and "being optimistic" were the names of my kidnappers.

I told her I didn't want to go back to work but I knew I had to. "Why don't you want to go back?" she asked.

"I don't want to leave Ted. I need him. I need to take care of him."

One of my favorite things Starla said was a response to me telling her that I am afraid to go out into the world again because I know myself well enough to know that I will grow. I don't want to grow away from Ted. She asked me if I could imagine where Ted is. Can I imagine that he and I are both going to keep growing? I loved thinking of Ted in a place where he is growing.

She also told me that she couldn't work with bereaved people if she didn't believe that love does not die. She thinks I am perfectly legitimate in thinking that Ted is still here with me in a new way, and that we will be together again when I die.

I told her about some of the experiences I have had lately that made me feel Ted was near at hand, just not visible.

"I expect Ted to have super powers," I said. "Can he give me patience with people I don't like but have to work with anyway?" She didn't say no.

After Ted's death, my mind dwelled between reality and fantasy about the finality of death. Over time, believing that Ted would have super powers morphed into feelings of certainty about the spiritual connection we would forever have with one another.

I have come to believe that mankind was never meant to understand completely the relationship between this world and the next.

I do believe that if we are open to it, an entire spiritual realm is available to each of us. Today I recall that when he was alive, we were certain that we were soul mates – two bodies with one shared spirit. On my best days now, I feel that same exact feeling of connection with him— undiminished by his death.

Starla asked me if I felt I could experience joy ever again. I said yes but only if I could share it with Ted. She said that over time I may find that sharing joy with Ted changes. I told her about lots of the things Ted loved and that we loved together. I don't know how I got started on that but I could have gone on and on for days.

There was so much joy in our lives together, and most of it was about peculiar things like racing the dogs into the bedroom at night so we could get a place in our own bed. I felt joy every night and part of that was knowing that Ted was feeling joy too.

When Ted was sick, it was a comfort for me to rub his back and make sure his side of the bed was warm when he got into it. It was a comfort to Ted to get his back rubbed and slide into warm sheets. This was our joy to the last day he was physically able to roll over in the bed for the back rub.

How can I find joy like that in this world…without leaving Ted behind? Starla seemed to think that it was possible that Ted would not have to be left behind. She told me she believes we will be together. I believed it at that time too, and I still do.

Writing letters to Ted and keeping a journal most days helped me feel as if I was working hard to bring Ted back. There is no doubt in my mind today that this is what I expected—Ted would come back if I worked hard enough. It turned out I was right, but not exactly the way I had expected.

At the time though, all I could think about was there was simply no possible way I was expected to carry on with my own life without Ted. It was like walking around without a spine or a head. Everybody knows that can't work.

I wrote to him every day. I just kept moving pen across paper. Moving pen across paper. This I can do, I thought, until all of this ridiculousness gets straightened out.

There was also the kernel of thought that if I had Starla to guide me, I would surely find my way. I even let the tiniest thought be heard that perhaps Ted was really gone and that's why Starla had been sent to me.

Eagle Visit

There was a particular Sunday when Caroline had arranged for all three of the kids to come over for a cookout and a work party to help me with the backlog of burning and cleaning up around the place. Unfortunately, it rained, so we ate inside and hoped for the weather to turn.

After lunch, the weather cleared a little. Caroline and I talked while baby Luke stared at the world from Caroline's shoulder. How does a young mother know to bop the baby around on her shoulder non-stop? Ben and Andy went outside without comment.

"Are you looking forward to going back to work tomorrow?" Caroline asked.

"I would rather stay home and try screaming a little more," I said.

Sometimes, early in grief, responses fly out of the mouth in a sarcastic blurt. No matter the subject of someone else's conversation, all you may want to talk about is pain and anguish. I'm pretty sure that is where I was at both mentally and emotionally on this particular day.

Caroline gave me a little hug as I cleared the table. I couldn't take my eyes off Luke, who was still bopping. He seemed awfully tiny still. Luke was born in December and Ted died in March, so the two of them got to know one another. I felt a shot of gratitude thinking about that.

There were times when I agonized over the futility of what Ted had to go through in order to fight his cancer, only to die in the end. But when I looked at Luke that day, I felt a glimmer of meaning.

I could see through the kitchen window that the rain had stopped. Trees were dripping, sunlight was filtering into a floating sheet of woodsy mist that lay about the tree trunks and the surface of the earth. A chickadee had arrived at the bird feeder and more lined up to follow. Everything seemed lighter.

As I loaded dishes into the dishwasher, I suddenly heard a fight going on outside between Ben and Andy. I could hear that the fight was about Andy taking pictures of everything he saw that interested him, and Ben was teasing him for it. If Andy was into photography or anything else, he was going to immerse himself utterly.

"So you are a photographer now?" Ben poked.

"Go fuck yourself, Ben. I know what you mean," Andy said. "Everything I do is a fad to you so I have to stop and get serious."

This short spat between the brothers felt like a return to normalcy. It lifted me up enough to go outside and work.

At four in the afternoon, a substantial burn pile was smoking up the neighborhood and burning very little. We had completely torn out a fence that had encircled the old garden. Caroline became emotionally unhinged by this act of destruction and retreated inside, with Luke riding on her shoulder.

Andy was dragging downed limbs from the woods with a great deal of gusto fueled by hatred for his brother's tormenting, acid comments. He stopped, then began to wander down the driveway.

For some reason I decided to walk into the woods and surround myself with the sunshine mist shrouding the ground and the trunks of my trees. Ben joined me there. "We are worried about you, mom," he said.

"Please don't."

"We want to help you," he said.

"You can't give me my life back," I said, and instantly regretted saying that. "I mean, don't get me wrong. I love it that you kids are close by and we are still together....but my life is gone." I could not believe I said it again. Did I want to tear my son into fragments for some reason? Is that what I did now – feel sorry for myself?

"We don't want you to be alone," he said.

"Let's change the subject, shall we? I see that Luke is progressing in the baby fat department. Do you think he is teething? I worry that Caroline is wearing herself thin."

"We all want to help you but we don't know how."

I told him to please not end the day with dwelling on an injustice and a cruelty that has ravaged all our lives. This comment struck me as particularly sad. I didn't want Ted's life to turn out to be a net loss. Ted's life was anything but that.

There was a commotion at that moment, and then Ben and I saw Andy running toward us. Caroline emerged from the house by the back door, staring at Andy as he ran, while moving forward with Luke now strapped to her back.

"Come quick," Andy said.

"There's a juvenile eagle in the middle of your street, Mom!"

I recall that on my last day of work before taking an extended leave to help Ted with his cancer fight, I saw an eagle hovering over my car on the way home. When I arrived home, I told Ted that I was scared he was dead, and the eagle was him, guiding me home to find his body. He said, "I'll come back as an eagle for you." After he died, I told the kids about it.

Everyone was jogging down the driveway toward the street. Suddenly I wanted to be someone else. In a rush of emotion, I thought I didn't want to look at Ted when he is not a full grown eagle yet, or is one, or whatever he might be.

But then I saw him – this gangly connection of joints with black feathers, hopping across the neighbor's yard and into the woods where his image dissolved into the mist.

I had never seen a juvenile eagle before that I could recall. Was that what I just saw? The kids were talking about what a juvenile eagle was doing on 258th Street – blocks from

the Stilliguamish River -- and I heard Andy say, "Hello Dad".
We lingered awhile without speaking.

It was almost dark then and I could see the moon and
a little star nearby. I needed to shoo my kids off my property
– my smoking, misty, lonely property. The sun was out of
sight although I could still see my hands when I stretched
them out in front of me. A strange and crooked peace had
taken me by the arm and was leading me forward.

This particular Sunday was a turning point for me.
All of us were suffering, not just me. The five of us were still
intact, in a new and strange way that we weren't accustomed
to. Seeing the eagle reminded me or illustrated to me how
close at hand love can be, even after death. I was not alone
that day. I would begin to have more days of not feeling
alone, mixed with days back to square one of life as a widow.

If there is one lesson I had to keep learning over and
over again, it was about the very nature of grief. It's ever-
changing moment to moment, hour to hour. It's quite
exhausting in its mercurial nature, its fierce speed and
directional changes. Early days of the hardest grief are spent
on a roller coaster. There is no escape. To anyone
experiencing this kind of grief, I promise you that it won't last
forever.

Leaning

I worked for a local government, in Human Resources. While the politicians at the top could be insufferable to work with for all the well-known reasons, I was lucky to have loving and caring, creative people for my co-workers. It was a gift to have them around me every week day. I felt surrounded by people who knew and loved my family, and I loved them for it. During this period of my life, I discovered that I had to let love in.

I widened the very small circle of people with whom I would share my truest feelings of loss and confusion. I was lucky to have Dani Mullaney, a strong administrator and gifted, world champion horse breeder. Among other acts of kindness, she acted as a screener of sorts, making sure my tasks for the day matched my moment-to-moment state of mind. I'm usually independent and I had to learn to lean on her, and others.

I tried not to be a downer to others at work. This turned out to be a silly thought. I found that talking about Ted out loud – the Ted we all knew before cancer took him – was a comfort to me and others. Ted lived. He didn't just die. And many of my co-workers knew him and loved him too.

Today I believe that even the most aloof and independent of widows will benefit from allowing love of these kinds of friends into her life – maybe a little more than she normally would have. For someone in the pain of grief, a workplace can be a sanctuary. In fact, I find that caring workplaces are where the most work gets accomplished.

Identity

After work, I would usually get home and spend very little time in the house before going to bed. I was dreaming every night. I lived to see Ted in my dreams.

I had a dream one night that granted my wish to see him. In it, Ted and I were living as hillbillies, wearing holey bib overalls and bare feet. In a ramshackle cabin we were cooking rabbit in a cast iron pot over a pot belly stove. I fashioned a nice lunch pail out of the rabbit skins. I skipped off merrily to work with my rabbit lunch in my rabbit lunch pail along a friendly dirt road.

About halfway down the road I began to realize that I would throw up if I really had to eat rabbit. I found a sneaky way to hide the fur lunch pail and its contents along a stone wall that abutted the path.

When I got home to Ted, I felt conflicted about this duality...I didn't want to be anything less than Ted and I had agreed we would be, which was to be hillbilly, honest and true. But I would gag at the thought of having to live as a hillbilly if it meant eating rabbit for lunch.

I woke up from this dream with one question on my mind. Who was I? I didn't know. I saw signs and clues everywhere, waking and sleeping. But who was I?

It's not uncommon for a widow who has built her life around her husband to have questions about identity, now that she is alone. Part of me had zero interest in finding out who I was if Ted was not there with me. On the other hand, part of me was somewhat inquisitive. There was a part of me that felt like a puzzle that needed to be solved.

What did the components of my waking life have to do with being a hillbilly and secretly hiding the parts of me that aren't hillbilly? I knew the dream was somehow a distortion of something important and meaningful, if only I could figure it out.

I finally settled on the realization that I was privately or secretly dealing with a terrible loss and simultaneously experiencing the transcendental nature of love and life and death. I was fighting against knowing who I was without Ted, and yet I could not help feeling curious about myself.

This period of being a widow was tiring, because there was so much going on in my mind. I was in constant turmoil down deep inside. My body ached all the time. I itched all over mildly but constantly, as if sleep deprived. That wasn't true – if anything, I was sleeping way too much. But I yawned a lot. At work, I could concentrate. Off work, I barely knew my own address.

Where I worked, there were fears of pandemic swine flu. One day I realized that I was fantasizing about death. I literally didn't care if I got swine flu and died. These thoughts were quickly followed by the realization that I couldn't die any time soon because my dogs and my kids needed me. Ted's death had caused me to know that wanting to die and being suicidal are two different things.

I have read much about grief and the stages of grief. Some say five stages, some say seven….theories abound. For me, there was a constant wrestling with conflicting thoughts and feelings about identity. I knew who I was before Ted's death when I was part of a duo. Now, I realized I didn't know who I was, alone. I felt curious about who I really was, underneath.

That sounds joyful, this curiosity and interest. But it wasn't at the time. It was a confusing and painful part of being a widow.

Money

Most widows face money problems. I did. There were little money issues at first that began a drip...drip...drip of more and then more bad financial worries.

For starters, a $200,000 life insurance policy Ted had with his employment was terminated five months before Ted died. We had the option of self-pay at $1,000 per month, which we could have managed for a year or so if we economized. But psychologically, it was unmanageable.

At the time of Ted's cancer, Patrick Swayze was also publically fighting stage four pancreatic cancer, and he had an active TV series. Ted and he were both on the same drugs. It really did seem to me that Ted was going to win over pancreatic cancer, just like Patrick Swayze seemed to be doing.

"Insurance companies bet you are not going to die," Ted pointed out, when we discussed what to do about continuing his life insurance. He also pointed out that the decision was mine, and mine alone since I was the one with a stake in the outcome.

I decided that I wasn't about to bet that he would be dead in a few months. I let the insurance lapse.

Thinking about Ted's realistic chances of survival would have been an enemy of our fight. Only becoming a widow could teach me a lesson on being realistic that is too late for learning. This was my first "drip" – the dawning of how expensive widowhood would prove to be.

The house needed to be re-roofed, and I was now undertaking that project. Once the contractor got started, he found board after board with mold from leaks up there. It was going to add cost to the project to replace the boards. Drip.

A lady from Westinghouse Hanford where Ted worked for ten years called to tell me that because Ted died two days before April, I would only be receiving half of Ted's retirement payout. Instead of receiving $36,000, I would be receiving $18,000. I immediately called an attorney that specializes in pension benefits, and after reading the fine print, he told me not to waste my money fighting.

I was angry not just about the loss of $18,000 – I was angry that the lady who called me could then go about her merry way in her life, while my life was billowing from a chimney, up in smoke. Drip.

My employment was unstable because I worked for Snohomish County. Snohomish County, Washington was like Shakespeare – no shortage of humanity in every light and dark permutation. I was the Human Resources Director, and I could be replaced at any time with a politico's girlfriend or boyfriend, or favorite sycophant, and I knew it. All of a sudden, with Ted's death, came actual FEAR of losing a job I now needed more than ever. Drip.

I found out that Social Security would not pay me a survivor benefit for six more years at a minimum. I was fifty-four and the minimum age for benefits is 60, and only pays if you aren't working. Drip.

Financially, I was now on a ship in high seas, rolling. My thoughts tossed back and forth between getting my arms around my near, mid and long-term money situation and trying to figure out the meaning of my life and Ted's death.

Many widows face serious financial losses when a husband dies. I was lucky in that our bills were somewhat manageable on just my salary, and I still had my good paying job. I refinanced my house, and got rid of extraneous expenses, like cable.

Hospice has many resources to help widows find professional financial advice. I recommend using these resources, as they can mean a great deal in the rebuilding of life on one's own.

I try not to look back on the financial implications of losing Ted. It just doesn't hold my interest. I don't usually focus on things over which I have no control -- although I would like to live in a country that has a favorable tax bracket for widows and widowers. The minute a woman gets separated by death from her beloved, she is abruptly shoved into the "single" tax bracket once more. The same goes for men who are left behind.

I was a teenager when I married Ted. I couldn't remember ever filing my income tax as a single person. I've had to learn the hard way that taxes are more expensive there.

"Living without you is not living," I wrote in a letter to Ted. "I can't just do my old life minus you in it with me and call it a life. I think I have to add something or some things to focus on. Temporary nuisances like the roof, the financial setbacks, and fears about losing my job aren't going to be enough."

Finances alone are very intimidating and can be frightening. Take advantage of advisors and resources. If you are like me, you'll find you need all your energy freed up in order to answer the larger questions of identity, and build a life alone.

Another Visit

On my way to work one morning I turned the corner at the end of our street and off to my right something rose and ran and rose and ran....it was the juvenile bald eagle the kids and I had seen on that cookout Sunday. It really did seem plausible that it was Ted, watching out for me. I pulled my car over and watched him.

I phoned Andy. He didn't seem all that surprised. He said that energy doesn't reduce or increase in our world, it just changes. The amount of total energy is a fixed quantity. Ted's energy went somewhere. He thought and I wanted to think Ted's energy was behind the unusual sight of a misplaced juvenile bald eagle at the end of our street.

What was it that I would say to Ted if that little starter eagle came up to my car for a few minutes and ask me how I'm doing?

I thought about famous searchers – people who lost a loved one and tried for the rest of their lives to contact them. Every culture, every time in history provides examples of the bereaved in search of love in the afterlife. I wasn't attracted at all to the idea of Ted as a ghost – although I did want him to come to me the way the ghost of the old sea captain came to Mrs. Muir in a movie from my youth.

I thought about Queen Victoria a great deal. I related to her loss of Albert. She wanted to die young in order to be with Albert. Instead, she lived forty years a widow. She never stopped wearing black. Her famous horseman, John Brown, was reportedly a spiritual medium between her and Albert. Who knows what is true or not true for other people? I hope anything is possible.

Houdini famously tried to find his mother for years, until he despaired over the false promises of mediums, spiritualists and séances that produced only false leads. In the end, he became a sort of undercover agent against the spiritualists of the day.

For a long time after Ted's death, I yearned to find a shaman of some sort, who could help me know for certain if my unusual sightings of eagles, strange coincidences and strong feelings of being near to Ted were true or imagined.

Today, I think back on the starter eagle the kids and I saw. Many other times, through birds and other creatures, I had felt Ted visiting me. What good do these visitations bring? A misplaced eagle was not likely to come into my bed at night and snuggle with me and be happy with me as we drift off to sleep in our happy little life, forever after.

At the same time, I have been filled with gratitude for the eagle sightings, and all the other creatures who visited along the way. I still get visits, feelings of a supernatural connection, or whatever they may be called. They all helped me inch forward, toward the reality and finality of Ted's death.

My advice to others who search: Believe what you believe. There is more unseen than seen in this world. Who knows where portals may be found? Whatever comforts, soothes, brings peace—believe.

Sleep

Most widows will probably find that sleep is either too easy or too hard to find. Most mornings, I woke up but didn't get up. It was my personal goal to drift back to sleep, unless I had to go to work. If it weren't for my job and the need to be a good role model for my children and to be there for my co-workers and customers, I'm certain I would have become addicted to sleeping pills. I fantasized about taking them every time I had to face another day.

At the same time, I yearned to be part of the world that was living right outside my bedroom patio door. Birds, grey squirrels, Douglas squirrels, chipmunks were everywhere outside, almost always going about their business in a drizzling rain. Inside, it was the opposite. Brownie, Tippy, Libby and Augie languished around the house, waiting for me to get up.

Grief sucks oxygen. Every part of my body was aching listlessly for a way to connect to the other parts of my body. What if I was going to stay together in this loose, unaffiliated way forever? Thankfully, the most powerful, sustained sense of disconnection within myself didn't last forever. I know now that it does subside, given time.

When I look back on how I moved through life in the first few weeks and months after Ted's death, most of what I see is not just the vicious pain of loss and grief, but a profound disconnect between the structures of my life and how I was operating within those structures. I was separate from my own self and my own life. Even today, I still have to work at it some moments. But early on, there was a shell of myself in the world, operating by rote.

I can tell you that eventually, as a new life emerges, sleep and energy return to normal, or to something new that will become the norm.

Security

Never before in my adult life had I ever worried about my personal security at home, until Ted's death. Not too long after Ted's death, two experiences brought the security issue to the forefront of my mind. I realized how naïve I was, and how my tendency to be open with strangers was no longer a safe way of being, all the time.

I was preparing to replace the roof, when an ad for gutters that blocked leaves caught my eye. I called the 1-800 number provided in the ad, and waited for a call. I wasn't disappointed.

Soon, a salesman arrived about six in the evening for an appointment with me to measure and provide a bid. He asked a few questions, then went outside to measure. Once outside, I couldn't see what he was doing from where I was in the kitchen. It was dark outside.

Alone in the house, I realized suddenly the totality I had told this man – this forty-something, somewhat rough looking stranger selling rain gutters. "Do you live here alone?" he had asked, among other questions.

"Yes. My husband died a few weeks ago."

With the man outside, roaming around the perimeter of my house in the dark, panic was now in my heart. I could see his flashlight beam as he made his way from one corner of the house to the other.

When the stranger came back into the kitchen, he began to fill out paperwork on the kitchen counter, while I watched. My mind was racing. I had a bright idea. "How much longer do you think this will take? I only ask because my four sons are coming by in a few minutes and I want to make sure they can get in the driveway."

"You have four grown sons?"

"No," I said. "I actually have six grown sons, two in law enforcement and the four who are coming by all work construction." If I was going to lie, it was going to be a good one.

Soon enough, the man provided his estimate to me and departed. Okay, I thought. I knew I had been lucky this time. He was unlikely to come back, knowing about my five mama-guarding men children.

My house felt haunted and creaky the rest of the night, and I didn't sleep very well because of my imagination.

A few weeks later, another security incident occurred. I decided to sell a wood chipper that was taking up a lot of room in the tool shed.

I listed the wood chipper for $400.00 on Craigslist. It will sell fast, I reasoned, because it's heavy duty and cost about $1,500 new. It's only three years old. It's been sitting idle, which would ordinarily be a concern. But before Ted died, he started it for me. At the time he said he was just "checking on it so I can use it later", but now I think he wanted to show me one more time how to crank it up.

The listing went up on Craigslist at 9 in the morning Saturday. A tall, angular red-headed man in his forties came all the way from Auburn to see it within an hour of the listing. "Yes, it starts", I assured him over the phone. I was pleased with my pricing due to this quick buyer coming from more than an hour's drive down I-5. I could feel four hundred dollars cash in my hands.

When he got out of his old Datsun pickup and cranked it up, that traitor of a chipper would not start! The dogs sat in a row like stair step orphans, staring in a transfixed state at the red-headed stranger as he pulled and pulled on the starter cord. The man peeled off his windbreaker at one point and put gas and starter fluid into it, and the chipper engine would start and bellow smoke and then sputter and stop. This went on for forty minutes with the dogs looking at him and looking at me and asking with their eyes: "Is this our new daddy?"

At last, I said to the man, "Just do me a favor and take it for free. Otherwise, I have to load it into my truck and take it to the transfer station and pay a toll to dump it." He agreed.

We loaded it into the back of his truck and that was that. As he was leaving he asked me if I was living here all alone and instead of saying something clever such as, "No", I said "My husband of thirty-four years died a few weeks ago. Before he died he started that chipper. I want you to know that. There was no billowing smoke and croaking engine when he started it. My dogs were there, so I have witnesses."

The man didn't know what to say. Who would? At least he didn't get out of his Datsun and slit my throat or some other gruesome, serial killer thing.

The Hospice contact most widows will have can probably help you find someone to assess your house for security. There are people at your church, at work, or even at your neighborhood hardware store who will help you think through security issues. There's undoubtedly a Youtube about it.

I've learned not to meet strangers alone. I don't sell on Craigslist if it means having a stranger come to my house. My neighbor told me he would list and sell for me, if need be. I don't answer the door for strangers. I have a deadbolt on every door. If I hear a car pull up, I go to my front window and confirm it's a friend, or kin. I keep a bottle of pepper spray by my bed, and one in my purse. I sleep with my cell phone next to the bed. I keep the doors locked, and the windows locked and blocked with a wood rod in the track. I joined AAA for the unlikely event that I have a flat tire, or a mechanical breakdown while in my car.

I'm snug now, battened down, and I feel safe. But I miss having a knight in shining armor by my side, and I would like him to take me back to the days when I was oblivious about threats to my personal security. Wanting to feel protected and watched over, and wanting to ensure my own personal safety, are two different things. I was starting to come to terms with the fact that I had lost my guardian.

50

Isolation

I didn't have the year Ted was sick to "get ready" for Ted to die. Knowing what I know now, I don't think there really is any way to be prepared for a loved one's death.

In my case, my entire adult life was composed around Ted. With his death, the center of my gravity simply plummeted, in free form and violent force, leaving me tumbling down and down and down. Nothing was holding me in place, intact. I was in physical shock for a prolonged period of time. I didn't know then that the state of shock would come over me in briefer and briefer waves for several years.

There was no need to think of Ted dying to induce deep sorrow and tears. No matter what I thought about, a force outside of my control spewed forth whenever it wanted, just like Mt. Vesuvius. Ted's death meant the end of Bridget and Ted World. I was constantly tripping over land mines of my former life. There was no schedule, no regularity, and no on or off button.

Another crummy new best friend of mine was isolation. I didn't want to return to work at first. I thought it would be unbearable to watch as others kept doing their lives when my life was dead. This is literally true, of course. Life goes on for others, even if you are stuck. I didn't know then that my existence as a stuck, dead thing was temporary.

The isolation that grief causes is multi-faceted and tricky. I saw others as disconnected from "the truth" about life, and that thought disconnected me from anyone who was not experiencing "my truth". This circular way of thinking was more isolating than junior high school, or getting arrested, or going bankrupt, or countless other ways we humans get severed from the sense of belonging to one another.

My life paradigms were literally shattered. I had held these truths to be self-evident: Ted and Bridget were born for each other. Ted and Bridget would most assuredly experience a fifty-year wedding anniversary together, which our kids would host. Ted and Bridget would die at or near the same time. Our adult children would have one super-size estate sale, since we both had many collections of vintage and antique relics.

The sudden realization that I was now essentially living a new and unfamiliar life was just one layer of isolation. Knowing that my old life would never return sent me reeling in waves of pain multiple times a day in the beginning.

Usually, after I was overcome with grief and had wept, I would be suddenly struck with ideas that were based in reality. For example, I had an intermittent idea that Ted might actually be a separate person from myself. It took years for that particular thought to take root entirely. Eventually, I did find myself as a completely independent person, although I am interdependent on the people I love.

Looking back on it I can see the way out of grief is carved while in the midst of grief. It's as if I was climbing a very steep mountain, traversing in vegetation so thick I couldn't see where I was stepping. Only when I reached the top of my climb could I look back and clearly see the path I took.

Give yourself some credit as you trek forward. You are on your path, however unfamiliar and disorienting it may be. You are on your path whether you want to be, or not. There will come a day when you will look back, and realize you were moving forward, even when you felt stuck.

Survivor Guilt

There is a lot of guilt for most grieving survivors. Holocaust survivors, war veterans and even long-lived people who have a chronic, sometimes deadly disease all experience survivor guilt. For me, survivor guilt was now a part of my daily existence. My mind was tumbling over little else.

I found myself preoccupied with being good, as in "a virtuous person." I didn't just love Ted and I didn't just live a life that was utterly entwined with his. Death caused me to idealize Ted in a way that was difficult to face, impossible to challenge. There was a guilt generator in the middle of all my grief, running high.

Trying to be virtuous enough to compensate for overwhelming feelings of guilt was not easy. The best I ever came up with amounted to imaginings of what a truly good person would do and think and say. Then I would do and think and say those things.

When Ted was first diagnosed, I was in despair because I thought he was good and I was not; therefore, we would become separated by death, and wouldn't be together forever. I told him that I am not a very good person because I only do what I think a good person would do. Ted said, "That is what every good person does."

A sinister ingredient of my guilt was a strong feeling that the wrong person was dead. It should have been me. I deserved it more than Ted. Today I still wonder if this wicked thought will ever completely go away.

My grief counselor, Starla, asked me what I wanted to do, what I enjoyed, what I liked. She was trying to help me visualize my own happiness, apart from the happy life I had with Ted.

Even though there are many, many activities and experiences I like, I remember telling her that I liked living up to an image of a good person. I enjoy being a good role model for my children. I want people to think I am a responsible person. I did admit to her I actually have to work at it. Ahead of me always is the "leader me" that tells the wretch in me what to do, think and say.

There was also the guilt in me that sprang from all the years of torment and anxiety that Ted put up with when he was alive and trying to love me. I saw myself as a hard person to love because I was always on guard and suspicious. The word "always" is usually an exaggeration, but there were times when this is what I imagined. I had killed Ted with my resistance to love.

At times in our marriage I really believed the only possible explanation for Ted to love me was that he must be trying to divine something out of me by loving me. These were the lamest of my thoughts since he never asked me for anything except my own happiness.

Does anything good ever come from survivor guilt? I think, yes. Survivor guilt sometimes allows we, who are bereaved, to stay close to our deceased loved one. This can make it difficult as we confront the guilt with rational thoughts. It helped me when I reminded myself that I am human. I, too, will die -- not on a schedule of my own choosing. There really are mysteries in the world and Ted dying ahead of me is surely one of them. It's no one's fault or decision who goes first.

Anger

Grief can have you doubled over in pain most of the time on the inside, while simultaneously upright and going about your day in a sort of normal way. With me it was a combination of being intermittently writhing inside from the pain of grief mixed with somewhat normal moments.

I went to a garage sale, something Ted and I did as a couple. I pretended Ted was looking at some stuff in a different area of the sale from where I was. I enjoyed picking out toys for Luke. I enjoyed just being myself in familiar and comforting pursuit, leading me to decide that pretending is undervalued as a legitimate grief coping skill.

In between being doubled over in pain, there is sweetness too. When I got home from the garage sale, I saw from my kitchen window that a Douglas squirrel had moved into the birdhouse that our friend, Dale made us years ago. "Did you see that, Ted?" I said, aloud. Bits of life were coming back to me wrapped up like Hershey's kisses. They were sweet.

One Sunday evening, I met my dearest friend, Susan in Mt. Vernon at the Olive Garden. Susan and Dale are a couple, and Ted and I used to go with them to the quaint northwest farming town of Mt. Vernon to eat or just hang out.

Now, Susan and I dined alone. I revealed some of my experiences with grief and the pain of not knowing how to move forward. I also realized in talking with her that I was deeply angry.

We placed our orders. Susan's dark eyes were staring at me, waiting for me to open up. I found myself letting it all hang out – expressing for the first time my rage. At this point, I was strangely focused on the compassionate nurse who was in charge of Ted's biopsy.

This plump and efficient nurse was all hugs and reassurances, saying at one point, "You just have to learn to take it one day at a time." If I had any doubt about what we were facing before she said that, I no longer did.

In my mind, from that point on during the biopsy experience, she was the one in charge of sign-ups for a class called "Give Everything That Ever Mattered to you to the Big Man with the Gun".

I explained myself just that way to Susan over dinner. Or rather, I think I spewed forth. I told her that I hadn't wanted to sign up for this dreadful nurse's class on losing. I didn't want to ever again see Madame Sign up Hugger. She was such a kind and compassionate nurse, I explained sarcastically. Little Miss Nursery Teach Me How to Lose My Life. I wonder now just how loud my ranting became at the Olive Garden with Susan that day.

Thank God for one close and forgiving friend, for all who are bereft.

I finished half of my mixed grill dish that was big enough for a St. Bernard. We hugged in the parking lot between her Impala and my Outback. I apologized for going off the deep end, so to speak. My dear friend would hear nothing of it, and we parted into what was now a dusky evening.

One would think I could drive home feeling deeply satisfied with my dinner and the company of my good and patient friend. Instead, I purchased some M and M's at a 7-11 store on the way home. I was either still hungry or very, very angry. I wasn't hungry.

Around ten o'clock that same night I raided the refrigerator and polished off the leftovers from Olive Garden.

This entire compulsive overeating episode reminded me that I used to scream all the time about being fat. Ted used to reassure me, by pointing out that he hadn't had to widen any doorways yet.

I was beginning to wonder if grief would kill me and bury me too -- in layers of fat. Why was I eating so much? Mercifully, I decided to forgive myself for handling grief in any way possible. I was trying to keep me from hating myself, which would lead to more self-destructive behavior. Handling grief on a day-to-day, hour-to-hour basis can be chaotic.

Before drifting off to sleep that night, I felt one more blush come to my face when I remembered how unraveled I became in the restaurant. For some reason, I started thinking about a long ago time when I was in a long line, waiting to use an outdoor bathroom in San Diego. There had been only one make-shift bathroom for the entire outside graduation ceremony of the Marine Corp boot camp Ben had been in.

As I drifted off to sleep after my Olive Garden outburst of anger and my M&M nightcap, I decided that widowhood was a lot like waiting in that line. There was nothing to do but wait for my turn at a stinking pit with no toilet paper. Widowhood seemed to be interminable in this way, and not something I would choose. I needed to lighten up and let myself spew forth every now and then.

If you are a widow, you have plenty to be angry about, no matter the details. I hope you will have at least one friend like my Susan to spew it to. If not, a clergy person or psychologist can be there for you. The more permission you give yourself to acknowledge and handle your anger in the best way you can, the sooner it will begin to recede. I don't know yet if it ever completely goes away.

Cancer

Widowhood is stressful enough without life continuing to move forward, which invariably brings new challenges. But life indeed does continue moving forward.

I found out I needed a biopsy on my right breast. I was pissed off that Ted wouldn't be with me. I was worried about the dogs and the kids if it turns out I have cancer. "Are there dark and foreboding clouds accumulating where you are?" I asked Ted in a letter. "I feel like I must have offended one of the gods. Maybe more than one." My buddy Guilt was always near. Had I done something to deserve all this?

I had used Ted's retirement cash out to roof the house, and this complicated project was nearing completion about this time. I told Ted all about it in my letters. "It's very thick and sturdy looking. If only I had a roof like that over my heart," I wrote. I wasn't kidding. That still seems like a good invention to me.

When Ted was alive, we were most often together. If we weren't together and something interesting happened to me, I would carry it with me in my mind like marbles in a handkerchief. I couldn't wait to spill it to Ted, whatever it was. I would spread it out before us both so that he could say things and I could say things, and somehow everything always made sense that way.

Being hit with the news that I needed a biopsy made me want to do that – only Ted wasn't as handy. I giggled a private joke to myself on the way home from the doctor. "I've lost my marbles," I muttered.

What surprised me more than possibly having cancer so soon after Ted's death was that I started to look upon this particularly scary moment in my life as an excuse to batten down all the hatches, to fortress myself for a fight. I already knew it was possible to survive the onslaughts of grief, coping, healing and more grief. I believed that I probably did have cancer, and that I would be able to face it alone. I was also beginning to realize that I actually wanted to survive.

Fight

I did have breast cancer. In June, I waited for my cancer care particulars and scheduling to come together. My care would be different from Ted's. His was a death sentence cancer, and his treatment plan was designed to slow death down for as long as possible. My cancer treatment plan was a curative plan.

I had stage one, HER2 cancer in the right breast. The plan was to have a partial mastectomy, followed by a year of Herceptin, a designer chemo drug I liked to pretend was made for just me, several months of Taxol chemo and an eight week daily radiation treatment. Dr. V.K. Gadi at Fred Hutch Cancer Care Center led my team.

While waiting for surgery and the other parts of my treatment to begin, I traipsed off to work every day to focus on other people's workplace problems and earn my living. During the day, the grief part of my brain was tied up and locked in a closet. As it would try to wiggle out of its ropes, another part of my brain would tie it up again. This second part of my brain was probably the part that wanted me to have medical insurance and money to pay the bills.

Chemo caused fatigue but I plowed forward by getting the chemo on Fridays, recovering Saturday and Sunday, and working my regular schedule otherwise.

Cancer treatment turned out to be a long tunnel I had to go through for one year. I did my year and still get frequent check-ups and mammograms, my care overseen by oncologists associated with Fred Hutch. I make it sound like a prison sentence that I served, and now I'm on parole and have to check in. I guess that's how I feel about it.

During the year of the treatments needed in order to destroy my cancer, a strange thing happened without my permission. I stopped grieving completely. I was sad about Ted's death, but the grief pain was literally vanished. I didn't even notice until later, when it returned.

Looking back I see clearly that grief takes all strength and energy. Likewise, cancer treatment takes all. The mind literally chooses for you which parts of you will work hard and which parts of you will be on ice for a while.

My mind chose to ice the pain of my grieving heart for a full year. I felt Ted close to me, because the children were with me most of the time while I healed, and we talked about him constantly. But for that year, my grief pain was at bay.

Alive

It was approaching two years since Ted's death when I finally completed all of my chemo and radiation. I was finished. I was breathless. "I can't breathe," I wrote to Ted on Monday night. I had quit chemo just in time, I thought. Chemo shreds your basics. Like breathing. Feeling things with your fingertips. Walking more than twenty feet.

On Tuesday, I arrived at work and someone saw me in distress as I left the elevator. I couldn't move except by inches. I couldn't breathe more than a tiny stream, which summoned an anvil on top of my chest. I shooed them away, got back on the elevator and haltingly drove myself to the cancer center a few blocks away.

I was put on bottled oxygen in the emergency room where my good friend Susan had arrived and was very distraught. My brain wasn't getting enough oxygen to be distraught for myself. But I was warmed by her presence.

I lay in the bed breathing bottled oxygen and had the strong awareness that I couldn't remember any aspect of the ordeal of the last two years that didn't include Susan here, supporting me.

Finally, I was diagnosed and medicated. I had bacterial pneumonia. Strong anti-biotics kicked in, and my breathlessness was replaced with a feeling of euphoria.

The bout of pneumonia following a year of cancer surgery, chemo and radiation left me feeling grateful and open and up for anything. I was tired, but I was alive.

That night I returned home about the same time I normally would have arrived. The minute I walked through the door, I broke down crying for Ted. *Where are you, Ted?* I was doubled over on the couch for a long time.

Active grieving had returned. The pain was unmistakable.

Part of Me

I healed from pneumonia. At home and in the car, I broke down uncontrollably, crying and in pain. I couldn't think straight, and it wasn't due to oxygen deprivation. I was actively grieving again. I wanted to be grateful, to get busy on my to-do list, to be productive. But, once again, I felt stuck.

One night, I awakened suddenly at the end of a haunting dream.

I was in some sort of labyrinth such as a house of many adjoining rooms with no way out. I didn't know why I was there. Without warning, two unknown men came up to me and told me they were going to slice me open with the steel knife they displayed, and they did. It wasn't a slashing. The knife went in very slowly and I didn't feel it. I thought about what I should do and I finally decided to face these two men and ask them, "What do you want from me"? I awakened.

Often, when I have an intense dream, I focus on how I was feeling in the dream in order to understand it. In my dream about the two men who slowly and painlessly sliced me open with a steel knife, I felt strangely at peace with the idea of being opened up.

Cancer had put grief on ice and now it was defrosted. This dream reflected where I was in my grief process, I realized some time later. I actually did want to be slowly opened up. But how?

I had been through the shock of Ted's death. I had wrestled with anger, money, shame and guilt, insecurity. I had learned a lot about how to be a widow. I had fought a year-long battle with my own cancer, and I had won. Pneumonia didn't kill me.

Every day for the last two years, I had figured out new ways to live as a widow without electrocuting myself or running into the garage with the Kubota. All the endless days and hours of lonesome yearning to not be in my situation while also figuring out how to deal with my situation were beginning to make sense to me. But I was still a grouping of fragments, strewn all over the place, not held together in any meaningful way.

My image was that every part of me had been packed into the back of a semi-truck/trailer, and the driver didn't realize he had left the rear door unlatched as he blew on down the highway.

The good news was that after two years of learning to be a widow, all the parts of myself were now tossed out where I could see them and arrange them as I wished. I just didn't know it yet.

Soul Survivor

Every time I went for a cancer follow-up appointment, I was given a survey to complete. At the two year check-up, I was completing my survey and for the first time ever I checked the box "yes" beside the question "Do you feel depressed?"

At this time, I was seeing Dr. Batson, an oncologist specializing in breast cancer in Everett. When Dr. Batson asked me to describe myself psychologically, I told him I didn't feel anything but gratitude about my cancer care. "Why did you check 'depressed'?" he asked.

"Did I?"

He didn't say anything. He just pointed to the evidence I had inadvertently left behind on my survey form. Finally I heard myself say, "I miss Ted so much -- even after two years this pain is so deep, there is a canyon running through me. There are echoes in the canyon."

Dr. Batson was merciless in that he continued to remain silent. "I'm falling into the canyon, or I'm about to fall," I said, then added defensively, "You're the doctor! You tell me!"

Dr. Batson departed, and soon I was talking with a mental health professional at the cancer center. I told her about Ted's illness and death, the hard times my kids were having because of his death and also because of the economic recession. I told her that I felt like a blind traveler in a foreign land. Where am I going? I don't feel I belong. I'm lost. I'm an object. "What kind of object?" she asked.

"Debris," I said.

"You are suffering from something called 'complicated grief'", she informed me. She went on. "Complicated grief is grief that happens to occur at a time of other profound loss and/or trauma, such as your cancer fight, the economic recession and the toll it is taking on your children, and the stress of working through cancer treatment followed by a walking pneumonia that could have killed you. Some people get complicated grief when they have been married a very long time, and the spouse dies."

"I have all of those things!" I blurted, as if winning at Bingo. I was instantly buoyed to know that the way I was feeling had a name. I might not be utterly lost after all. This mental health person recommended anti-depressants and participation in a weekly group in Everett called "Soul Survivor". I hate support groups, I thought. That thought was followed by a small voice inside of me that said go. I was trapped by depression caused by complicated grief. This two-pronged prescription might show me the way out.

On the way home from that appointment, I thought about Ben, Andy and Caroline. They were adults now. Ted and I had given each child of ours both roots and wings. I didn't know that losing them to adulthood would hurt me like a skin graft. My skin, grafted to their wings. That image made me laugh out loud in my car. My very soul now has stretch marks. Again I laughed about those ribbons of silver that skate down the slopes of my breasts and belly – the marks of childbearing and breastfeeding that were etched upon me, many years ago. Sometimes there just isn't enough vitamin E.

In a benignly grey cement-sided office building on Colby Avenue, down one flight in an elevator to a basement, along a stretch of hallway with closed doors that have only numbers, there is a conference room with several long metal tables pushed together into a ribbon, with metal chairs along both sides. When I opened the door for the first time, there were only strangers there, silent and mostly hunched over in different ways, closed chests, tear tracks on young faces and old faces, and a white haired lady about my age, wearing a denim vest over a white blouse who said, "Welcome," to me as I entered.

"Is this the Soul Survivor meeting?" I said.

"Yes. Please come in and have a seat."

A Ghost Community of the Bereft

On my first visit to Soul Survivor, I wasn't asked to give any information about myself. The lady in the denim vest was there for logistics and was the one who unlocked the door and brought Kleenex. She had been called by Hospice to let her know a woman named "Bridget" would be coming. Soul Survivor was sponsored by Hospice, and only the bone fide bereft could attend by referral. It always strikes me as strangely comforting to be recognized as bone fide at anything, so I sat down.

I was invited by a man in his thirties wearing a pale yellow shirt and Dockers to share as little or as much as I liked. He turned out to be the facilitator, and I'm pretty sure he was somehow connected to Hospice. He was definitely the pastoral type, so if I did talk, I knew I should definitely not say things like, "I hate my fucking widowhood." He didn't do any praying, so I decided to stay.

Another man, in his sixties or so, shared with a strange gusto about the things he and his wife liked to do. He had white hair and a white, waxed up handlebar mustache that ended in a curl on each side. His clothes made him look like a Swedish man, or a retired lumberjack. I have no idea where those thoughts came from, but when I looked at him, I felt I was peeping into his past and that's what I saw.

He said "Life is for the living," several times as if he were teaching kids. Or maybe it was defensiveness about the fact that he told us he was moving in with his deceased wife's sister. This man made me think things like, "What have I gotten myself into?"

Someone else spoke, and said they were "Picking it up from last week." Even though I hadn't ever been to a meeting before, I understood what this lady was saying. "I keep my television on all the time," she said. She was a tidy crier, weeping big, easy tears into a linen hanky. She seemed to be about my age. I found her quite beautiful to look at, and I don't think she was wearing any makeup. She was a natural beauty. "I need the company," she said. "The sound of the TV is comforting."

Another woman spoke who said she was still not ready to believe her husband had died. He died at her feet when he dropped from a heart attack on their way out of the Sears store in Mt. Vernon two weeks ago. They were married sixty years and it was her birthday the day he dropped.

Being witness to this particular woman's grief nearly peeled my skin off and left me sitting there, raw. She had an antique, translucent face and bloodshot eyes. She couldn't weigh more than eighty pounds and sat swallowed whole in the tan trench coat she was wearing to stay warm. I wanted my pain to be more like that. I felt she deserved every tear and there was not a whiff of guilt or regret. Just grief.

When Ted died, an invisible blanket separated me from the rest of the world. Now I knew that others were under the blanket with me.

"I wonder if our newcomers want to say anything," the facilitator man said. I didn't pipe up. A man younger than me said that his wife had died one week ago. She had cancer and they had just gotten married. That was the extent of it. He didn't come back ever again, at least not during my time there.

Apparently time ran out at this first meeting I attended. It had been an hour. By the end of that first meeting, I felt like I had been cooked in an oven. I wasn't hot but I felt like I was cooked to a turn and ready to be devoured. I wasn't raw anymore. It was a unique feeling, as if I was participating in a sacrifice of some sort that was both pagan and spiritual, depending on your point of view.

Soul Survivor had turned out to be some sort of exquisitely painful and abstract emersion into a ghost community of the bereft. I had been plunged into a dark secret, then I walked out into an ordinary day, onto the sidewalk in downtown Everett where life is cruising around at 25 mph on Colby Ave.

I could feel the wind whistling down that canyon inside of me. For an hour on this particular and unforgettable day I had been intimate with the private pain of other people. For an hour, my pain wasn't lonely. What a strange relief it was. Instead of air, I had breathed in the grief of others, some grief as new as frost on a rose.

Over the next six or seven visits to Soul Survivor, I discovered that there are no rules, or identities, or expectations in Soul Survivor. The group exists of the grieving, for the grieving. Ted had been gone more than two years, and when I first shared with the group that he had been gone two years, I expected to be flunked out and expelled because it had been so long. But I was not.

I was with a different group of people every session. Some were known to me from previous sessions and some were newcomers. There was a sort of rotation in and out of this otherworld. The bereft came and went as they pleased. No one batted an eyelash over Ted being gone over two years, nor did they look at me in wonder when I said that there was a part of me that expected him to return.

Two women will remain vivid to me forever. One woman was in her thirties with four children under ten years of age. Her husband had died suddenly three days prior. Not a job injury and no life insurance. She couldn't speak and her sister came with her and told her widowed sister's story. She who had lost her husband came to cry and be with us and I left the group before finding out if she could ever speak on her own behalf. I will never forget her.

Another woman was what I would describe as seeming the most lost. She appeared to have everything in the way of independence, but she also appeared to have no emotional means of processing what had happened to her husband, who died of cancer. She and he believed that God is a myth and she didn't believe her husband was a spirit or in any other state other than rotting flesh. No one tried to persuade her otherwise. She was just there, lost. She may be there still. I expect to see her again someday, kicking a can down a road as a means of filling the hours. Or maybe killing them.

Soul Survivor had a profound impact on me. Death comes calling in every circumstance. I was not an adult when I married Ted. I only got to know myself as part of him and his life, our life. Ted was not here to help me in the world any longer. I knew solidly that I had to keep figuring it out for myself, because he wasn't coming back. I would be living with the sadness as it came from nowhere and kicked me around. I would be learning to live with....live with....live with. We were together for a long time and had a good life together. One of us had died. One of us was alive, bereft, waking up on a daily basis and deciding how to proceed.

Tippy

Thinking about myself alone and what I truly wanted was new, but it was happening. I never knew the freedoms of adulthood outside my marriage to Ted. I didn't always give in to Ted's wishes – far from it! But if I "got my way" in our marriage, the winning took away from the enjoyment of whatever it was I had won. Most of the time, Ted and I were pretty skilled at "wanting" something that we both guessed would be what the other wanted. But now I was alone.

I didn't think Ted would like what I had in store for our property. This had been our sanctuary. To keep the dogs in, Ted installed a fence across our property, with a gate that I now found more than a little annoying.

I decided to install a short, decorative fence, three feet high with one flat top and one dog ear alternating. It would carve out a smaller yard for the dogs. Most importantly, the installation would free me from that front gate Ted had been particularly attached to. I wanted to enter and leave my own property without having to fiddle with a gate.

The appearance of this line of thinking – about the gate and many other aspects of my new life -- marks the moment that I realized Ted and I still shared only a spiritual bond. I wished it could be true that we shared a physical bond, but we did not, and it was final.

I can see that this was a turning point for me. I knew I was alone physically, and I was in the driver's seat of my life, with no passengers and no co-pilot.

In the coming weeks, I hired the teenage son of a trusted friend to dig the fence holes for my little fence. He set the posts and ran stringers between the posts. I cashed in my credit card points for a Lowe's gift card and used it to buy cedar boards. I cut my own wood, and nailed it up…one flat top and one dog ear, alternating. I threw open the front gate ceremoniously, feeling triumphant.

Ten minutes later, I watched one of our dogs, Tippy, scale my new fence and escape across the street to my neighbor's manicured lawn and into the woods. My fence was too short.

I tried a gazillion different ideas to keep Tippy behind my fence, but Tippy was an unrepentant fugitive, much like the charming Paul Newman in the movie "Cool Hand Luke". Unfortunately, Tippy was charming only to me.

My across-the-street neighbor was furious when Tippy got into her space. The mother of two pre-teen boys with a firefighter hubby, my neighbor worked herself to the bones making everything about her exterior life perfect. She was entitled to the perfect lawn and garden beds she worked hard to tend. And she was unflinching about making complaints.

Even though her husband told me he didn't mind, his wife had property rights on her side, and I had my futile efforts and apologies. Ultimately, she won and I went back to the gate across the driveway.

I wasn't as good as I should have been at closing that gate all the time, and this led to more friction. Years later, for many reasons including a dislike for my unsympathetic neighbor, I sold my home and property in Arlington in order to let all the conflict – both internal and external -- go. Getting to that point was part of my grieving process, part of learning how to be a widow.

Thank goodness for my grief counselor, Starla, who had given me permission to forgive all the decisions that didn't work out, and even the ones I might come to regret such as building a too short fence.

Building the little dog ear fence wasn't a waste of my energy, money and time, in spite of providing the opening round of Tippy versus my neighbor. Building the fence opened a door in my heart, and started a renovation in there.

However long the journey, whatever the means, every widow will find a way to move forward. She may remarry. She may strike out on her own. I hope that every widow will awaken to a day when she feels free to choose which path to take, and free to move forward.

New World Order

I began to say goodbye to writing letters to Ted. Or maybe I was saying a type of goodbye to Ted, using letters. Either way, after I quit going to Soul Survivor, I found myself not writing to Ted as much.

Around the three year anniversary of his death, I wrote to Ted two more times, and then I stopped writing to him altogether. In my next-to-last letter, I wrote, "The pain of losing you is getting a little easier to live with. I am not running away from it. It hurts, but I believe it more readily now -- that is to say, I have lost you and it's irreversible. It really happened and you are truly not here physically any longer...at least not in your old Ted suit. Squirrel suit, maybe. Maybe an eagle suit. But not the old Ted suit."

I had already let go of many physical objects that were from Ted, about Ted, or representing my life as defined by what I sometimes now refer to as the "Ted and Bridget Show".

Together, we collected art, mid-century ceramics, antique clocks and many, many books. One of the last items I gave up was a nostalgic oil painting of a little boy with his horse. When I gave this present to Ted, I said it reminded me of the boy inside of him that was still there.

I was often fighting with Ted about his childlike nature, because I felt he left me holding the bag of the disciplinarian, the organizer, the adult, in our relationship.

But I also loved and cherished Ted, my life partner and soulmate.

Ted had collected Maxfield Parish, but now I found myself wanting a particular Charles Wysocki cat print. It was sort of silly -- cats on a shelf with library books. I began to be attracted to art that had a naïve kind of light hearted energy. My heart knew that I had to fight gravity in every way I could.

For the next year, I spent most of my free time sorting out, bringing in, painting walls, changing furniture. I see this period now as part and parcel of my discovery project of who I was without Ted by my side. What would make me as happy as possible, in this new world order?

Spirituality

Because my life with Ted was over in so many earthly, tangible ways, I began thinking along spiritual lines more frequently than I ever had in my life. I wasn't thinking about shamans or séances anymore. I wanted to feel my own internal spirituality, because I knew that is where Ted was dwelling these days.

I remembered that God in my original family was a cheesy, tacky thing to talk about and it was reinforced in my upbringing that God was definitely a taboo subject. Now, I had absolutely no spiritual framework other than scholarly biblical metaphors I learned when I went through a process called "confirmation" in the Episcopal Church.

My parents thought Episcopalians were more intellectual about the whole enterprise of creation and morality, so that's where my family of origin went when going to church seemed like the proper thing to be doing. My parents were mostly responsible people and parents, and they also worshipped the false gods of keeping up appearances. But spirituality was another thing altogether, and I craved it both near me and in me now.

I spent a lot of time working through the conflicts between religiosity, morality, the superficial appearance of virtue and spirituality. The sorting of these particular subjects are still inside my head and heart to this day. Seeking can become a collection, too.

"Dear Ted," I wrote, in my last letter to him, although I didn't know at the time that it would be my last. "I am moving forward sort of. I realize that there are two kinds of being. There is 'in this world' being which is my situation. Then there is the 'crossed over into the spirit world' being, where I can find you now – and only there.

Naturally, I want a bridge between the two worlds that looks like the golden gate or the trestle from Marysville into Everett that I cross every work day morning and in the afternoon after work. Surely I will succeed in having you by my side if I build a spirit bridge to you. I am hoping that you can communicate with me in a way my spirit can interpret."

I told him in this last letter that I was mightily pissed off that I had to go to bed alone at night. Pissed off that I won't get what Ted had….a warm bed to retreat to in my last days. He won't be rubbing my back at the last.

At that moment I realized that I had done that…..my care with the help of Andy had made it possible for Ted to die in his bed, and not have to go to the hospital. This realization brought me a strange sort of pride. Ted's achievement of his desire to die at home was not a consolation prize, as I had felt for the years since he died. It was a profound and meaningful gift – one that I had played a key role in providing.

There was deep regret that emerged in my mind while writing this last letter. I thought a lot about all the times I was enraged at Ted. I would rant and scream and cut him to smithereens with my words. It sometimes felt like Ted dying and getting to move on while I had to stay here and feel stuck was my payback.

I wrote: "Please hear me. I am sorry. I am creepy mean when I am angry and feeling used. Feeling used is what you might call a major issue for me. It keeps coming up. That's probably because I'm pretty certain my parents brought me into this world in order to get something...maybe youth? Distraction? Hope? Whatever it was, it didn't pan out for them. They ended up like two cats trapped in a pillow case. And I turned out to be a little big mouth opinionated civil libertarian with a chip on her shoulders. And then you adopted me. Thank you."

So, there it was. I was a confused kid when I met and married Ted, and now I was confused and starting out in life all over again. I didn't feel the need to write to Ted any more after that letter, probably because I had finally worked out the totality of my situation.

I now felt certain that he was part of the spiritual world, unseen, but present in my life, nonetheless. I didn't feel the need to write to him anymore because I felt him beside me always.

I speak with him silently when I am with other people, and out loud at times when I am alone. I still don't know if he can grant me wishes and control outcomes in the physical world – my best guess about that is that he cannot. That doesn't stop me from asking him to intercede when I want a particular outcome I have no control over. But I do know I feel loved by him. More. He makes me feel loveable.

Today, Ted has compassion for me, and he helps me cope with my life. Reaching out to Ted spiritually aids me in accessing my own instincts and wisdom about my own life as a widow, a woman who is nearing the end of middle age, a worker, a friend, a mother and a grandmother, and whatever I may become.

Crummy Friends

Going on four years after Ted died, I called the 1-800 number for Wellspring Family Services, the employee assistance contractor for Snohomish County, my employer. Calls to Wellspring go to a distant state, where every call is screened for a referral to a suitable counselor or community service. "What is the issue?" I was asked by a disembodied Wellspring voice.

Just what was my issue? I had to count all the monkeys on my back before I could answer the screener. Empty nester. Widow. Cancer Survivor. Fed up worker. Make that disoriented worker – I had recently been fired but then I wasn't fired, so I had some issues with my employer.

Nothing seemed to help me feel better these days except buying, hoarding, eating, and then regretting metric tons of M&M's, with chips and ice cream chasers. "Compulsive overeating," I said to the screener. Eating too much was, after all, my oldest and dearest crummy friend.

It took months to tell my counselor, Sharon, everything about myself. There are a lot of tangents in counseling. It takes forty minutes to get warmed up enough to start spilling your guts and in two or three utterances, your time is up until next week.

But slowly, my story got spilled out. Sharon asked me over and over if I have enough power....yes, I have enough power. Enough freedom? Yes, I have enough freedom. Enough love? Yes. Plenty of love. Enough fun? I have no idea.

I left my parents….either rebelling against them or trying to emulate them…then I was adopted by Ted. We built and protected and loved a family. Now that I am alone, I have only the vaguest notions of what I desire, what I really want, what makes me happy, or how to have fun.

This counseling illuminated for me that Instead of having fun, I tend to distract myself. I don't really enjoy myself as much as Sharon recommended a human being really ought to.

She sent me home one day with an assignment to draw my pit. My pit was basically the depths of my overeating self. I drew a standard V-shaped, rounded bottom pit, and loaded it up with M&M's, chips, tater tots, ice cream, and peanut butter…all my crummy friends were there. On an 8.5 X 11 inch piece of Xerox paper, my pit drawing was roughly 5 X 7. A second assignment was to draw myself on the same piece of paper in a manner that depicts where I live in this pit. "Me? Get into the pit?" I said. "You don't have to ask me twice to get into my pit."

Always the gracious audience at my show, Sharon laughed at my antics and sarcastic wit, and she laughed at my funny pit remarks. She and I both knew I use humor to armor myself. "You'll have fun with it then," she said.

I drew stairs in the pit. I drew my exaggeratedly long right arm on step three or four from the rim of my pit and I was pulling myself up from the bottom of the pit.

Until I drew my pit and myself in the pit, I had no idea how close I was to escaping my pit. By the time I stopped going to see Sharon, I had drawn in a few good friends, vacations to the Oregon Coast, art, music, and my dogs just outside the rim of my pit. Sometimes I use these and other fun resources to distract myself, and sometimes I choose to go into my lousy pit with my crummy friends.

I selected a different counselor, Joan, to help me figure out what to do with my life. She pretty much came to the Sharon conclusion that I didn't know how to enjoy life nearly enough. From her, I learned about something called Pinterest that she thought would inspire me. It did, and I now have a respectable hoard of art supplies to prove it.

Joan's approach to my food issues differed in that she had me stock up on all my binge foods and then she gave me permission to eat them without guilt until I didn't want them anymore. "Any connection between food and trying to be virtuous will cause a compulsive eating episode every time, without fail," she told me.

From Joan I learned that being virtuous was both something I craved and something I was suspicious of and loathed. By the fourth anniversary of Ted's death, I was a little less virtuous about everything.

I definitely knew I wanted to leave my job. I had stockpiles of Ben and Jerry's ice cream in my freezer but I crawled into my pit less often than I used to. I bought a fancy camera and treated myself to a grizzly bear safari vacation on Vancouver Island.

Remarkably, the Ted and Bridget show had by now produced six grandchildren.

Remembering Blue Skies

One of the most powerful lessons from all the counseling I received was the realization that had Ted not died, he would have lived. I had no way to ever know how our lives would be progressing and what problems we may have faced.

We had purchased land and were going to sell our Arlington house and build on our land in eastern Washington in 2010. But what would the recession have done to those plans? We may not have been able to sell the house or secure a building loan. What if Ted and/or I had been diagnosed after our move? Would we have to sell out and move back to the Seattle area for the best care possible?

The point is that I'll never know. It doesn't rationalize Ted's death to think of these intimidating possibilities. But it did help me put my grief into a little wider perspective. I had nothing but blue skies in my imagination when Ted was diagnosed and subsequently died, so that is all I had to compare. Somehow, this idea brought me a twisted but very real and long overdue bit of peace.

My life was bigger now because of all the new grandkids. My loneliness was bigger now, too.

Arlington was half an hour to an hour away from my kids and I felt left out. Tippy was escaping regularly and my perfect neighbor lady from across the street was in my face quite a bit about it. I felt accused just driving toward my home every night.

Something was always going wrong with my property and the house was cold because it was too big. I was in touch with my misery like never before, but at least I could name it now. I knew I wanted to be a needed part of my family and not just someone that everyone comes to visit. I needed a smaller house and less property to care for. Tippy needed a yard with a fence.

I started becoming attracted to the idea of living in Edmonds, a little artsy town on Puget Sound that runs ferries to and from the peninsula and hosts some kind of community event every weekend. Edmonds was fifteen minutes from both the Andy and Ben families, and a half-hour away from Caroline's family. I didn't want to live in anybody's hip pocket, mind you, but I did want to be an active participant in family life.

When I thought about moving away from Arlington, I didn't know if I could let such a huge thing go as I had with so many of the elements of my life with Ted. I didn't know if I could bring myself to leave the Ted and Bridget home in Arlington, to create a new home for myself in Edmonds for the person I was becoming.

Match Dot Detour

It was the early summer of 2013, more than four years after Ted's death. I told the kids I was planning to sell the Arlington place and move to Edmonds, and the earth tilted slightly. Just when you think you know your mom....It's hard to be the mom your kids expect you to be when you decide to uproot your entire existence in order to build a new life.

They nor I had any idea how far I would go to find out what I really wanted for myself. What if I made an irreversible mistake along the way? I justified my decision by saying simply that I was lonely and needing to feel more connected. I didn't want to explain that I also felt lonely because I was too connected to what amounted to a too-big ghost ship of a home, with its acres and outbuildings and memories in every square inch.

Loneliness is in the brain as well as the body. It's more than an ache or an itch. Loneliness can lead to deadly consequences for some such as suicide, heart failure and depression, to name a few.

I had my roommates of sort in the cat, Augie and my beloved dogs, Libby, Tippy and Brownie. They helped me through Ted's death and they kept loneliness at bay the better part of most days. I thought I had loneliness fairly well accepted, bottled and corked. My plans to sell out and move were the most ingenious inventions of my loneliness prevention plan yet. That's what I thought, although I knew deep, deep down, I was winging it. I was winging everything.

One day I came home from work to find my pet sitter, Dana, waiting for me. I knew something was wrong. I saw Brownie's body, lying in the far eastern part of the property. She had died in mid-walk, of a stroke or heart attack. Dana had stayed with her until I got home. Now I had to bury another loved one and learn to live with the searing pain of loss once more.

Caroline and Luke came over to console me while my neighbor helped me bury big Brownie by the garden. She was so big, we had to hoist her in the bucket of the Kubota.

That sad night I rattled around the house, got on the computer to check for the latest home for sale listings in Edmonds, and registered for Match.com. If that last part reads like a non sequitur now, that's because it was an unplanned, down-the-rabbit-hole foray that I still can't quite reconcile with my image of myself.

How do I explain that when Brownie died, loneliness in my brain made my hand reach into my wallet and give Match.com my credit card information?

Many years ago, at my request, Ted had taken me to a porn shop in Pasco, Washington. I had never been in one, and back then they were still a taboo. When I walked into the establishment with all its black leather and rubber genitals, I was in shock, a haze, having an out-of-body experience. I just couldn't believe that there were retail stores with fake penis's and fake vaginas lined up on shelf after shelf like hammers at the Ace Hardware.

Back then, I had quickly darted out of the porn shop and spewed laughter at Ted in our VW bug, all the way home. Logging on the Match.com almost forty years later put me in an identical state of disembodied amazement. All the pictures of people seeking pictures of other people!

They had profiles, just like the ballpeen hammer, the claw hammer....Whatever I wanted, here's a tray of men in my area who want to give it to me. This time I wasn't laughing with Ted in our VW. I was alone on my burgundy loveseat with two grieving dogs and an indifferent orange cat, and I was typing out my search parameters.

I wrote that I was looking for friendship and the companionship of a man who was honest and true, with a burley build and a beard. I was flexible, but that exact physical type was my preference. If you are in a suit, you're out. If you are a jock, you're out. Family man, get over here and let me take a look at you.

I was looking for someone who wanted family life the way I did, had been widowed like me if at all possible, with adult kids not living at home with him, and a job or retirement from a job. I wanted someone who would cook for me and not invite other people.

I stayed on Match.com for two weeks. I got many hits from men whom I'm pretty sure were in prison or on parole. I got some from men I didn't like the looks of. Most men aren't widowed, I came to discover. My filter, I realized after about a week, was really screaming "Is that you, Ted?" Consequently, everybody got a reject from me.

I wasn't really wanting a Ted sub. I wanted Ted. I closed my account and didn't ask for my money back. I didn't want to go through the hassle and, in fairness, I got my money's worth of understanding myself from those two weeks.

Match.com cost me about the same as a couple of sessions with a counselor. And it helped me figure things out. I wasn't lonely in general for a man in my life. I was lonely for a particular man named Ted Clawson, and no other man would do.

I was a widow for four years and then some. I had just told my kids I was selling my rural Ted and Bridget home and moving to Edmonds, which is most certainly not rural. I had just come home from work to find a dear friend and companion dead on the ground.

Hoisting the carcass of a loved one into the bucket of my Kubota had opened widow wounds more than just a little. For a couple of weeks, I was hurting from grief all over again, every day.

I can see now that I joined Match.com because I wanted to go back in time and make all of the losses in my life add up to a new and wonderful adventure with Ted, the love of my life. I joined Match.com for two weeks to find a lifetime reprieve from pain. There is no such thing, of course.

For me, being a widow has meant a parade of consolation prizes, and Match.com was a two week experiment in wanting to win again. Almost forty years ago, life gave me my happily ever after. I was alone and on my own now. There would be no going back, only the yearning to do so.

It was revealed to me that there is no such thing as a replacement happily ever after. I had to find a way to live with me in this world and Ted in the next, with a spiritual connection between us but not a physical one.

Maybe there's a rule somewhere in this world that once you win the grand prize of love, you're ineligible for another grand prize. I don't know. But once I clicked off on Match.com I knew for certain that the detour was over. I needed to get back on the road. My road.

Edmonds

One day in March, 1990, I had been promoted to department head of the Human Resources Department of Snohomish County, Washington. I had looked upon this job as my reward for going to college nights and weekends while pregnant, while lactating, while raising three kids and building a good life with my husband.

Our kids know about Dr. Seuss because of Ted. But for years when I would read to them before bedtime, it was from a textbook of some sort. They were interested in whatever it was I was reading to them because I read with drama and enthusiasm. I also wound up making great grades on tests this way.

To celebrate my new job accomplishment, I had splurged on a new, green, Ford F-150 pickup truck for Ted.

Twenty-three years later, I drove that same truck to and from Goodwill fourteen times, with its truck bed filled to the brim with the stuff of thirty-four years of married life. I was downsizing big time. I was scaling a life lived in well over 3000 square feet down to a 920 square foot, mid-century, three bedroom, one bath rambler built in 1964 on a half-acre, partially wooded lot in Edmonds, Washington. The house was across the street from a wooded park with trails and no streetlights or playground. I knew it was perfect for me, Libby, Tippy and Augie the minute I saw it.

I moved into my new place the day after Christmas, 2013. It was then that I realized the magnitude of my decision

– the house was sitting on a foundation that would need to be gutted, re-enforced and re-insulated. The kitchen and bathroom would have to be gutted and rebuilt. There were no gardens, just an expanse of grass and chain link fence, with a slope of woods full of mountain beaver.

The plumbing fixtures leaving the house were cast-iron and sagging from age and would need to be replaced with PVC. My neighbors could probably hear my alarm go off in the mornings, they were so close on one side. It's one thing to read about a fixer-upper, to fall in love with a fixer-upper, and another thing entirely to move into one.

I spent my first night as an insomniac buried under the covers. I thought I heard rats. I thought I heard someone breaking in, or living in my attic, or living in my dirty crawly crawl space. My dogs thought we were on vacation and that I had rented a smaller house this time. "And by the way," they seemed to be saying. "Where's the ocean?"

I immediately thought of moving back to Arlington, where my old house was being painted and made ready to go on the market. It wasn't too late! But I had learned the hard way over almost five years that there is no going back. Those first few sleepless nights, I realized that I was like one of those settler women whose husband drowned in the river halfway to Oregon. I had to stay with the wagon train and keep heading west, whether I liked it or not.

I had become in my own mind, "that brave widda Clawson who done lost her man and kept right on a'goin'." That was me.

My too--close neighbor turned out to be someone I knew who had retired from Snohomish County, Ken McCauley and his wife, Sue. Nice people, both. Suddenly my unease about how close they were became a comfort for security reasons... They were quiet and I was quiet, so our closeness has never been a noise problem, or any other type of problem. It was just something I hadn't encountered before, so I feared it at first.

There are people who paint, demolish, build, pipe, roof and overhaul your space according to whatever you want. There is Pinterest to show you what is possible. I had fun designing, making trips to Lowe's, budgeting my projects, building a garden, and tamping down the tunnels that mountain beaver tend to build overnight.

I divided my woods in half, mentally. I claimed the front half, and mountain beaver got the back half. My neighbor at the top of the hill thinks they are cute, so the mountain beaver have that going for them.

My house in Arlington was ready to go on the market in March, and then an unprecedented mountain slide happened in Oso, Washington, just up the street from Arlington. As a consequence, there were suddenly no buyers for the Arlington area. Everyone was afraid of that area now, and it took until late summer for prospective buyers to determine that my acreage was not on a slope or beneath one.

It finally sold, but for a lot less than I had hoped. My old lesson of letting go of theoretical money came in handy once more. I do not allow any what-might-have-been calculators into my life anymore. I keep moving forward.

Another Money Lesson

At the time I sold the Arlington house, I had been a widow for more than five years. I didn't exactly give Andy the truck, but I gave it to him to use as a down payment on a new car for himself and his family. Then I started seeing it every day, because it was parked in front of a store on a road I had to travel up and down to get to I-5 and my job, every day.

"Hello, Ted," I said every morning. One day, I looked up and near the truck there was a bald eagle perching on a wire in front of a Fred Meyer store, right in the middle of town. "Show off," I said.

I told my bosses at work that I wanted to semi-retire in May of 2015, and take a three-day-a-week job doing nothing but training, investigating, and employee relations – all the activities I love that aren't connected to politics at Snohomish County in any way. It seemed strangely comforting to me that I enjoyed doing things that nobody else wanted to do, like training managers, hearing complaints and working through difficult employee issues.

My bosses agreed to let me make my move to this part-time job, and the timing couldn't have been better. A dishonest, snake-oil-salesman-type council member was running for Executive and I knew that things were going to be very dirty from that point forward. My plans were snagged a bit because of this man, but eventually I was able to semi-retire in October, 2015.

I thought I wouldn't have to have anything to do with this new Executive or his cronies since I was too far down the food chain for anyone at that level to care about. I was wrong about that, and decided to retire from Snohomish County employment forever in February, 2016.

If you have made it all the way through my widow lessons thus far, you may realize that I've lost quite a bit of money as a result of losing Ted. There was the lost life insurance. Ted's retirement payout was cut in half because he died on March 29 instead of April 1. My Arlington roof cost a lot more than anticipated. I lost equity in our Arlington home because of a catastrophic geological mudslide nearby. There were other, smaller financial losses and disappointments. There is no tax bracket called "Widow", for example. Because of the tax implications of being single, my own income had been reduced when Ted died. Now, I had quit a good paying job that I enjoyed entirely, just to get away from a sleazy politician.

One of the biggest regrets I have in my life is that I worried about money so much that sometimes I made choices because of money that distanced me from what I really wanted. I was angry at Ted a lot while he was alive for what I euphemistically called "working below his potential". He was a licensed, professional geologist who chose to work in road maintenance, making far less money than he could have. I felt I had to earn as much money as I could, and I resented the fact that he placed his happiness above income.

Ted was a hard worker who loved working outdoors. He rejected the allure of making more money in an office in exchange for being happy. He encouraged me to do the same – to follow my true heart's desire -- but I lacked courage.

It was only after I had lost everything that I realized how very little money I actually needed to be happy. If I have my family close by and Ted's presence in my life, then a 920 square foot cottage, a garden and a patch of woods are enough. This time, I learned my lesson in time to enjoy it. But I also feel the pain of regret for my criticisms of Ted, and for not learning my lesson while he was still alive.

I have already discovered that Ted is in my life as so much more than a mere ghost, and yet one of the biggest widow lessons I have learned is the ease with which such guilt does haunt. But then when Ted was alive, I was blissfully unaware of how everything could be lost in a biopsy.

When I think about regrets, I cry out for Ted to help me. I literally say something such as "Please help me. I'm so sorry I ranted at you all the time about money. I feel so bad." In death, his hearing is improved, and I am eased back into my pursuit of happiness somehow by him.

I told a friend once that I wasn't the type of person to take his ashes to a restaurant and order him a meal along with my own. But Ted Clawson is with me everywhere I go, nonetheless. And having him with me all the time is free.

The Last Phone Booth in Edmonds

These days I enjoy being creative, and I spend a good deal of time writing. My son, Andy, plays my muse at times by feeding me clever lines to spring from and use for inspiration. One day he said something about "the last phone booth in Edmonds", and I took my writing from there. I wrote:

The Last Phone Booth in Edmonds

In downtown Edmonds, I was walking beside my son, Andy, and his wife and three children. The youngest of the three, Theo—not quite two—was riding Andy's shoulders. Julian and Bella, at seven and five years of age, squabbled about something. I too had three children and each in their turn rode the shoulders of the daddy they worshipped, the man I adored.

It was just me now. My beloved husband, Ted, had been dead five years. This particular day happened to be our thirty-ninth wedding anniversary.

"That's the last phone booth in Edmonds," Andy said, pointing to a phone in a niche on a pole by the sidewalk on the south end of third. "Mysteries abound there," he said. He tried to make it sound spooky.

There is no beige in Edmonds. The town feels accidentally quaint and carefully cultivated. I had moved here to walk on the street and look at vegetables and crafts, smell sea air and not be in Arlington where Ted and I spent a quarter-century raising our family. The move had been a thirty mile maneuver to a different planet. I wanted the Puget Sound for a neighbor. I wanted less triggers for the broken parts of my heart. I downsized from the out-loud-life of five to a 1964, 920 square foot one story house on a quiet street across from a nature park.

"What do you mean, 'the last phone booth in Edmonds'?" I asked.

My question went unanswered due to a chaotic shift in our walk. Andy had downloaded Theo. Theo had started a short squall to half-heartedly protest the download. Julian and Bella were pleading with anyone who would listen for relief, each from the other. Sara, my daughter-in-law and mother of this brood, announced that we were at the Gelato shop.

"Anyone who wants gelato has to behave," she said. She is a hundred pound, small voice, power pack of a woman, so we all listened up.

"What did you say, Mom?" Andy asked me.

"I said I was over-identifying with your mysterious phone booth."

After gelatos, I peeled off from Andy and his tribe. I walked to my car on sixth. I like to park on sixth because it is close to the coffee grinder stand at the Saturday Market in Edmonds. The coffee I buy is called "Back Pedal Brew." I call it my

"Crack Pedal Brew" because I am addicted to that particular coffee. I have two cups every morning to kick start my day.

On the way home I was thinking about coffee – probably because I could smell my bag of the stuff resting on the passenger seat. But I don't remember actually arriving home. I didn't pull into the garage that I can recall, or let Libby out to do her business, or let Libby back in, or lie down to treat myself to a Saturday nap. I only remember the smell of the coffee and the weight of the phone receiver in my hand as I tucked myself into the phone niche on third that Andy called a booth. "The last phone booth in Edmonds," he had said.

I felt the receiver in my hand, snuggling my ear. Whenever I feel snuggled, I think of Ted. And then I heard his voice as it spoke to me through the wire.

"Are you still there?" Ted asked.

"Yes and no," I said. "I don't think it's wise for me to talk with you like this. I'll just cry myself to sleep tonight and I won't tell anyone about it and that will just add to my isolation."

"Maybe you are isolated," Ted said.

"But I moved to Edmonds to end my isolation. I'm with family a lot. I stay busy. I don't want to cry myself to sleep," I said. It's true that I don't like to cry – in bed at night, or anytime, really. "I don't like to engage in pointless activities."

"When you are alive, crying can be a way to tell yourself how you really feel," Ted said. "That's why it's embarrassing for most people to cry in front of others. Who wants to reveal something about themselves to themselves in front of spectators?"

I could feel night air against my back, a gentle muscle tension in my shoulders. The skin of my hand was a ghostly violet under the street light. I noticed the thumb is curled back and pointing at me. I didn't have many questions for Ted, I noticed. Everything seemed clear to me, although I did hope no one saw me. That would be embarrassing.

"I don't know what to do," I said.

"I know."

"The overwhelming weight of so many days ahead...I don't know how to dream anymore. I'm stuck."

"You are stuck in the last phone booth in Edmonds."

"Yes!"

"That's really not something I can help you with," Ted said.

After Ted said he couldn't help me, I found myself walking back up to sixth where I believed I had left my car, although downtown Edmonds looked different at night than in the daylight. I really wasn't entirely sure where I was going.

I walked to my car, then past it and kept walking to Main and then the library. A man sat on the brick ledge in front of the library and I sat down beside him.

"Would you like to pet my dog?" the man asked.

I pet his dog, although I never liked Chihuahua dogs. Still, I pet the man's dog.

"Are you wandering?" he asked. "Have you ever heard the saying that all who wander are not lost?"

"Yes."

"Yes, you have heard the saying or yes, you are wandering?"

"I'm not a wanderer," I said.

The night sky was black, with stars visible. It was a crisp cold night now. Everything in this late night version of Edmonds was absolutely still and silent. I walked down the hill from the library to third and returned to the phone booth. I brought the receiver to my ear and leaned in. "Everything is meaningless without you," I said.

"I don't have any answers for you," Ted said. I heard him sigh. How strange it felt to hear Ted sigh and how it pierced me, reminding me of the truth I want to avoid, even more than the onslaught of my own tears in bed at night. I was leaning in, stiffly, cold, wishing for one more sigh. "You are alone essentially," he said.

"I really am a wanderer now, a kind of hollowed out lost and wandering woman standing in the cold night air in the last phone booth in Edmonds, talking with my dead husband…who isn't helping me, I might add!"

I heard him chuckle. God, I loved hearing him chuckle.

"Good night," I said.

I walked up the hill to sixth and got into my car and started home. The man at the library was walking down sixth now, with his dog on a leash. They were headed north. I drove south to main, then east toward home. Libby was waiting for me by the kitchen door. She was animated, her long hair twitching and her one good eye looking both at me and into me with appreciation for my being.

There was no explaining to Libby--or to anyone else--where I had been, or where I might be going next.

The End

I wrote this short narrative after I had been in Edmonds about eight months. I was busy with home remodel projects and with living near the water, enjoying the fairs and festivals of the area and spending time with my kids. When Ted first died, it was as if there was an invisible blanket between me and the world. I slowly let a few others in under the blanket with me, but feelings of isolation are still part of my life.

The isolation of profound grief eases by half every year or so for me. That means that it will get smaller and smaller, but it will never completely go away. It's a part of me. I have incorporated the widow lesson of greeting my grief when it appears, almost every day. Just because it is there doesn't mean it gets in the way necessarily. When sometimes it does disrupt my life, I have to actively withdraw from my life once more, and grieve.

Grieving now means crying unexpectedly, usually when I am alone. Or I may have the feeling for a day or two like I've got the flu, only I know it is just the muscle aches of grief.

I sometimes find myself thinking about moving to a town where I don't know anyone or anything, just to be around strangers and away from everyone who knows me. Those kinds of thoughts appear at first to be something I should consider, and then I realize it is grief wanting me to run away so that I will be alone again, under my invisible blanket.

Much of what I write about these days is somehow connected in some direct or oblique way to my broken heart, which may be mended back together, but will never be completely intact again.

I very much want to help other people who are experiencing grief, and I don't have to look very far. At work. At the store. In a church I found that I liked enough to return to. Everywhere, someone I encounter is in pain because of loss and grief. If I can help, I help.

That's what writing *The Widow Lessons* has been about for me. In a way, I'm still writing it.

Afterword: Other Voices

I completed the writing of The Widow Lessons in February, 2016. I decided to include the voices of other widows in my area. I felt certain that other widows would provide additional lessons for widows who are searching for a way to live with the devastating loss of a life partner. I was right about that.

I reached out to my local newspaper and a regular columnist – herself a widow – wrote an article as a shout out to other widows who wanted to share. I will always be grateful to Julie Muhlstein, the columnist who wrote the article, for helping me connect with others. Their insights follow.

D's Story

My conversation with D started by her telling me that she didn't think she could add anything to my book. She said that hers was not a good marriage and the story of her husband's death was not sweet. She and her late husband were married sixty-six years. D is eighty-seven now.

"We only shared an emotional connection when he was dying," D told me. "He was vulnerable, and all of his defenses were down. I could finally see his humanity."

I didn't probe for details about her marriage. Nor did I ask for details about what she described as "his horrible death" at age eighty-eight.

I asked D to describe her grief experience. There was no shock, but a disorientation as well as a sense of "lostness" and empty space, in spite of being prepared. She used the word lostness, which I had not heard before. A good word, I decided.

She talks with her late husband now, for they did share similarities in topics of discussion. She thanks him when the car works, for he was the resident mechanic. She discusses politics with him in these talks.

What I learned from D is the truth about life and death is sometimes much different than the media version, the obituaries, and family statements. There is a fertile field for lies in all of these things, D stated to me, and I agree. I also learned that D experienced grief pain "for him, and the pain he felt and experienced in dying." This helped me understand the intense pain I still feel, when I think about everything that Ted lost at the end of his life, and the pain he suffered.

I am confirmed in my belief that whatever a lifetime with someone has been, grief is still grief. Pain is still pain. D had the lostness, the empty space and the pain that has also been part of my experience. She came to acceptance quickly because of the circumstances around his death and the facts of their long marriage. But pain came to her, nonetheless.

One pang inside of me when I spoke with D was around talking. She said that she made sure everyone in the family – including two children of the marriage – talked during the pending death of her husband. I know my children talked privately with their father about his dying. But I never did, because I was too absorbed by my personal need to deny the fact that I didn't have the power to save him.

MJ's Story

MJ has been widowed twice. Her first husband died and she was left to raise four children on her own. She described the financial struggle that finally led to her going back to work part-time. She said writing down her thoughts helped her deal with the pain.

Being responsible for her four children helped MJ stay focused on the tasks of the day. This distraction from pain was part of what helped her keep moving forward.

Nothing, she said, helped her more than the "cocoon of love" that wrapped around her, made up of family, friends and strangers.

After the loss of her first husband, money came to her as gifts in cards from complete strangers as well as people she knew. Everyone did what they could to support her and her family. Her neighbors bought her a stereo and some records. At night, when she couldn't sleep, she was able to listen to music to comfort herself.

The second time around, her husband died after many years of marriage. They truly lived, she told me. For a time they traveled Europe for six months. They lived on a sailboat for years. They had many adventures together. When he died of Parkinson's disease, she was once again surrounded by love of family and friends. This time around, her grief came with some regrets, however.

MJ described the hospice room her husband died in at Providence Hospital in Everett as a horrible place of bright lights and bare walls. It was a thoughtless place in the midst of a modern hospital. She regrets that she did not insist her beloved die at home. After his death, she talked with Providence about it and they are trying to raise money to improve the room. Still, she lives with regret.

Today, her little dog Joey brings her great comfort. She's able to live comfortably in a low rent apartment that includes assisted living. MJ is eighty-eight now.

Hearing MJ's story of grief made it clear how much love is available to us, if we are lucky and if we let it in. I have a hard time letting other people surround me with love, and I think many widows have that issue. We tend to play hostess, even in the midst of grief. I wish I had been more like MJ, allowing myself to be in a cocoon of love when Ted died. I did the opposite and isolated myself, as many widows do.

MJ struck me as the kind of woman who lets nothing of value go to waste. She let love in to surround her, both times she was widowed. She played music on a record player that was a gift, and hearing music was her comfort during long and sleepless nights alone. Financially, she has made adjustments in her life with part-time employment and affordable housing. Going on ninety, she keeps moving forward. Her losses, her grief are part of her.

Barbara's Story

Barbara lost her husband of thirty-four years in 2007. Before he died, she was able to write the words she would read at his memorial service. She read parts of it to her husband, in his last days. She hopes he could hear her. I think, yes.

She observes that others had expectations of her, and about how she would move through her grief and act. Before his death, she lived happily. How could she know how to live now?

To others she offers some lessons she has gathered along the way. She said her mother had two sayings that helped her. "Do what you gotta do" and "Not today". In other words, her mother gave her permission to consider what she wanted, rather than live up to others' expectations of her.

She recommends forgiving yourself for whatever "should's" or things done or undone. Be kind to yourself. She believes from her experience that the people who truly love you will wait in the wings, so to speak, for you to move forward. The best friends, she says, are those who let you talk, reminisce and remember as long as you need.

She, too, was visited by eagles. At the exact moment of her late husband's birth, on his birthday, came an eagle overhead her deck. It lingered there as she and her family were toasting her husband, on his special day. Her husband had often packed a stuffed eagle with him for every visit to the hospital. Today, eagles are extraordinarily important to Barbara and her family.

In her letter to me, Barbara included some quotes. One struck me as particularly helpful. "We are all broken," wrote Hemingway. "That's how the light gets in."

Victoria's Story

Victoria told me that she and her husband had an extraordinary connection. When they would walk into a room, others could feel the love between them. In November 2015, he died. She told me that since then, she has been "wandering through life aimlessly."

For two years, her husband had one close brush with cancer after another, some of which led to his paralysis and ultimately his death. She has a huge support network and says that she is never alone, but always lonely.

Like so many widows, her husband handled all the finances. Now, she is fighting to keep her house amongst a multitude of other financial complexities. She says she is simply "out of gas".

Still, the serious, practical obstacles and problems are bad….but the grief is worse to deal with. "Sleep eludes me. I wish I could stop crying," she said.

Victoria points out that there is so much written about the "stages of grief", it gets tiring. There is, in actuality, no rhyme, reason or schedule to it. In fact, it gets irritating hearing about what is "supposed to happen, and the timetable."

Victoria expressed the honor she feels in caring for her late husband through the long journey that ended in his death. "I wouldn't change a thing," she told me.

Pam's Story

Pam and her husband had been married forty-six years when he died of a massive heart attack while fishing. I like the way Pam relayed her journey to me. To me, her format was in the style of "laying out of the bones" of where and how grief moved her. She wrote:

A few notes on what was most helpful to me in "getting through"

1st year – attended two different Grief Share groups weekly

Went to weekly counseling

Weekly shared grief with a small group of friends

Told the story of my husband's death over and over to friends who were willing to listen

Went to vacation home only several times during the year – took friends with me

Tried to surround myself with supportive people

Made sure that I had plans for holidays with family or friends

Shared my "husband's birthday" at a location that he loved with his family

2nd year – attended one Grief Share group weekly

Went to counseling about once a month

It was about the third year before I was able to resume yoga and walking – I didn't have the energy, prior to that time

3rd year – went to vacation home by myself

4th year—bought a condo – will be moving soon

At the time that Pam wrote to me, she was embarking on a trip to Tokyo to be with family.

Kelley's Story

Kelley lost her husband of thirty-four years when he was fifty-four and she was fifty-two. He died in the prime of a healthy life, of brain cancer. That was two years ago, when she and I communicated.

I commend her for seeing a therapist during his illness and after his death. She says that it saved her life because what she was experiencing on a daily basis was overwhelming. The hardest thing she ever did was care for her husband, which meant watching her love and life mate die from such a terrible disease.

Kelley told me that her husband was in a coma three weeks at the end. Every morning she had to wonder if he had made it through the night. "Not knowing if my husband was dead or alive—I cannot tell anyone how that feels emotionally, day after day," she said.

His words, "I don't want to die," haunt her to this day because there was nothing anyone could do to stop the illness. She compares how she feels now to the effects of post-traumatic stress disorder. That felt like an apt description to me.

Kelley told me that she had lost her dad, a sister, and a niece. But for her, nothing compares to losing a husband. "Your identities are so intertwined by life that you really do feel that half of your identity is cut away." She said she has always been fairly independent, worked full-time at a great job, and had many wonderful girlfriends and family that were close by. She describes herself as being alone, but not lonely.

She and her husband were just starting to enjoy their empty nest when cancer struck. She still feels married emotionally, so she keeps well-meaning family and friends at bay by telling them she is "content". Her loss is such that she does not think her grief has an expiration date or deadline, no matter the good intentions of friends that are out there for her.

Kelley is satisfied for now to come and go as she pleases, eat a lot of cereal for dinner, and do things in life that bring her joy. She says that she feels blessed because her husband left her both mentally and financially okay. After his death, she moved from acreage to a condo, and visits the best part of her life – her daughter – on the other side of the country.

Joanna's Story

Joanna's husband was terminally ill with colon cancer for two years. "It was supposed to be six months," she recalled when she spoke with me. He never wanted to be put back in the hospital, and she is glad she was able to be with him when he drew his last breath.

"Foreverness is so much," she said. "Once you become a widow you realize you had no clue what it means to be a widow. For one thing, it's the absolute end to your life as you knew it." She was fifty-three when he died, and it's been twenty-years since she became a widow.

After he died, Joanna says her husband came to her in a dream in which he was "vividly healthy," telling her that everything was going to be alright. She was greatly comforted by this vision, and the message. However, widowhood has taught her many painful lessons.

Because she and her husband did most things together, her life today after twenty years of widowhood is dramatically different from her life with her husband. Everything changes – from cooking, to hobbies, to work, to friends. Her life is a procession of changes, and she predicts that it will continue to be.

To the newly widowed, she recommends three things. You will live moment-to-moment for a long period. At some point, try something you enjoyed before you married. Stay open.

Gratitude

Julie Muhlstein's article in the Everett Herald brought the stories of more than forty local widows to me. It was difficult to know which ones to include, although there were common threads in all of them. Listening to the experiences of others once again helped me to heal another inch or two.

Those common threads include the weight of grief, and its infinite implications, as well as a spiritual and emotional tempest. Most widows realize at some point that their life is over and not over. More than one widow used the words "slogging through," "lost," "wandering," and "haunted." The heaviness of grief comes from carrying and learning to live with the loss of a life partner – no matter what that has meant to each – and the necessity of living in the present.

Most widows feel their lost love close by. Most talk to him. Spiritual beliefs vary from widow to widow. However, I didn't talk with a single widow who felt a specific belief system spared them at all from the unique grief a widow experiences.

No woman I talked with found any one book or pamphlet helped her. Therapy helped some. Talking with another widow helped most. Many widows credit one friend or family member that allowed her to tell and retell the story of her husband and his death as being instrumental in helping her from the tightest of grief's grip.

From the writing of "The Widow Lessons," and the stories of other widows, I have derived a strength to wake up. I strive to make the best I can of my new life. I know now that every day, I will connect with Ted in some way, be it words or the natural world on display in Edmonds, Washington. I do believe that being a widow has taught me additional ways to see.

Made in the USA
Las Vegas, NV
05 March 2022

45072483R00075